I0049116

PENNY STOCKS

Penny Stock Trading Secrets for Making Money
Investing

(How to Trade and Invest in Penny Stocks to
Achieve Financial Freedom)

Charles Walker

Published By John Kembrey

Charles Walker

All Rights Reserved

Penny Stocks: Penny Stock Trading Secrets for Making Money Investing (How to Trade and Invest in Penny Stocks to Achieve Financial Freedom)

ISBN 978-1-77485-268-2

All rights reserved. No part of this guide may be reproduced in any form without permission in writing from the publisher except in the case of brief quotations embodied in critical articles or reviews.

Legal & Disclaimer

The information contained in this book is not designed to replace or take the place of any form of medicine or professional medical advice. The information in this book has been provided for educational and entertainment purposes only.

The information contained in this book has been compiled from sources deemed reliable, and it is accurate to the best of the Author's knowledge; however, the Author cannot guarantee its accuracy and validity and cannot be held liable for any errors or omissions. Changes are periodically made to this book. You must consult your doctor or get professional medical advice before using any of the suggested remedies, techniques, or information in this book.

Upon using the information contained in this book, you agree to hold harmless the Author from and against any damages, costs, and expenses, including any legal fees potentially resulting from the application of any of the information provided by this guide. This disclaimer applies to any damages or injury caused by the use and application, whether directly or indirectly, of any advice or information presented, whether for breach of contract, tort, negligence, personal injury, criminal intent, or under any other cause of action.

You agree to accept all risks of using the information presented inside this book. You need to consult a professional medical practitioner in order to ensure you are both able and healthy enough to participate in this program.

Table of Contents

Introduction

This book provides actionable advice on how you can make investments in penny stock as well as trade penny stocks, and earn money from the process.

Stocks are one of the most effective investment options around the globe. And it's not just high-value stocks which cost hundreds, tens, or thousands for each share. even if you choose to invest in shares that are priced at less than 10 dollars or under $5, you have an excellent chance of making lots of money through the process, specifically with capital gains. If you can't afford to put aside 10s or 100s, even 1000s in dollars for each share, then perhaps these penny stock investments are your best way to take. Even if unfamiliar with the world of stocks trading and penny stocks specifically it is possible to learn all there is to know about them and be successful at this. There's a lot of potential for earning money with penny stocks. This book will help you understand exactly what you have to accomplish.

If you're among the people who believe you must be a pro at trading for investing in penny stock, you're wrong. Like all other securities and stocks need that you are well-informed and disciplined. You must also have good strategies when participating to be successfulwhich is exactly the purpose of this guide to help you do. It will give you the information that you'll need to start your career as trader in penny stocks. It will also provide you with a detailed guide of the best ways to trade and calculate your profit and avoiding the risks of penny stocks and more!

This is the place where your penny stock's successful journey starts.

Chapter 1: Penny Stock Basics

Contributing to the community is something that a lot of people are eager to do. They must be aware of the extent to which their money will be able to generate and many even want to see if they can do this as a day-long job. There's a myriad of speculations you could create. Some people prefer to are cautious and keep their money in an investment account , while others choose to use an retirement plan. Certain people will choose to invest in land and choose one of these options in the event that the market is favorable while others prefer to start a businesses, join the stock market, or invest their money to a friend who is looking to explore new territories. The options are endless regarding the possibility of launching a new investment, and choosing the best one for you is the most difficult part of starting.

One type of investment you may want to consider could be the Penny Stock. It's a kind of stock that starts low, and is priced at around $1 per one of the options. According to the Securities and Exchange Commission in the United States, a Penny Stock will be traded at around $5 per offer, however many of them would be much lower than the price.

A penny Stock could bring a huge profit for those who know how to make use of it, but it's nothing other than a well-known option because it is based on the typical Stock market. It is often employed when a company requires a significant amount of money. It is possible to suffer massive misfortunes regardless of whether or not you purchase at a low cost or not. However, should you are able to peruse the market, you have the chance to spot many opportunities and earn some decent profits at the same time.

The best way to ensure that you're not getting into a serious mishap with these stocks is to be careful about whom you purchase from. There are some shady individuals who make a large purchase of Penny Stocks so as to increase the price. They'll use fake websites, public statements as well as Stock message blocks and other means to increase about the Penny Stock cost so more people will purchase, but then the price rises more. Then they will sell the Stocks for the increased price, earning them a lot of money but everyone else will not have the opportunity to locate buyers and will be forced to grab the Stock or dispose of it in the event of a disaster.

Luckily, the Penny Stock must follow some guidelines in order to avoid the cycle described above, also known as'siphon dump'. In

US These Stocks have to have a price in terms of market capitalization, as well as the least value for investors. Remember that no matter if the stock you take an interest in is priced below $5, it isn't considered a penny stock unless it's a part by an exchange like the Stock Exchange.

The Benefits of Penny Stocks

We spent a bit of time exploring a selection of aspects to be aware of when trading penny Stocks in the hope of being able to invest funds into these opportunities. If you're cautious about monitoring the market and watching the trends before you purchase and you should have the ability to determine if an alleged siphon and dump scheme occurs. In the event that you feel that something is going up in value too rapidly, and you discover that there was only one buyer of a large number of Penny Stocks with only one firm, or you feel that this person is trying to get someone to buying something which doesn't seem to be the best option, it's a good option to choose an alternative option to Penny Stocks. It is a good thing you can make money with Penny Stocks however you must keep your eyes on the ball and make sure you're not trying to rush into something that isn't a good fit for you or comes with a lot of cautions in addition to it. The best way to profit from the Penny Stocks you own is to know what you want to find out prior to buying any shares.

There are many things you have the chance to look into regarding a Penny Stock prior to beginning. For instance, you can begin by looking through the website of the business you wish to collaborate with. This gives you an insightful idea of the company due to the fact that lots of information is available. The next step is to examine the Balance Sheet of the company to determine the amount of obligations it is managing. If there is many obligations, the business could try to sell Penny Stocks to escape obligation however should they don't know how to handle this obligation, throwing more money at them will not help. You should select Penny Stocks from organizations that have a profit or which can be able to reduce their financial losses and will not take on the burden of having to run.

Penny Stocks are a fantastic way to contribute in the event that you're hoping to begin with an alternative , or want to expand your portfolio in order to make your money and work harder. We will look into more aspects of Penny Stocks and the ways you can choose to use them to your advantage.

As such prior to getting into the fundamentals of trading Penny Stocks, we have take the time to learn about the different ways companies can use to show their expertise in this kind of market. Be aware that, while there are rules and regulations for Penny Stocks, they are not considered to be part of the Stock market . Therefore, dealing with them is different from the norm. We will examine how an organization could make a list on Pink Sheets as well as what that means to you as a financial expert.

Listing in pink Sheets

To allow an organization to start by introducing Penny Stocks, they will first need to record their Form 211 so as to be recorded on Pink Sheets. It is a privately held business, which is different from the alternative (which we'll discuss in a moment) that is the over-the counter Bulletin Board, which is an aid provided through the NASDAQ. There are many companies that use Pink Sheets to work with and, when they complete their Form 211, they should send it with OTC

Compliance Unit. OTC Compliance Unit. The market maker is expected be in charge of the publication for the company. The seller and the expert can choose to offer an estimate of the cost for the company, so it is a simple one. There are, however, certain companies that will not be focused on this simplicity since they will not present their current figures on the financials of their business.

For the companies documented using those Pink Sheets, you will discover that they're usually small-scale arrangements. They don't need to collaborate with the SEC for the exchange time and won't be required to keep track of their reports on a regular basis. At present, some organizations record their activities to demonstrate what they're doing and enable the financial professional to feel more comfortable investing resources into them, however it's not required. A lot of times it can be difficult to gather the information needed to be able to recognize those companies included on the Pink Sheets since you simply do not have the information which is required to start.

Advantages of Trading Pink Sheets

Despite the fact that companies that use Pink Sheets are not needed to keep simple records or make regular updates, a finance expert will typically find some excellent options to swap Penny Stocks using the help of Pink Sheets. You are likely to be receiving a high yield because these are the stocks which are difficult to manage. There are also businesses that are part of this group. They were previously solid, however for some reason or other, they had to abandon the substantial trades due to an urgent need they could not have the capacity to meet. They could even be acceptable exchange partners to trade with, and you can reap several great gains from this.

It is also possible to find dark companies that you can trade with to help them progress before they transition into one of the major trading platforms. There is the possibility to join these companies in the right time, and it could earn you a an enormous reward when they develop and then move on into trading on the Stock Exchange.

Furthermore What's more, the Pink Sheets framework has a structure that allows you to differentiate between organisations that are in the. This allows you to determine which stocks are more risky and which have a more likely to fail based on the classifications established. You can choose the risk setting you're at ease and happy with, but as a novice it is essential to know which belong to each class in order to aid you in settling on a selection.

If you're planning to use Pink Sheets as a feature of your exchange strategy it is essential to make sure you conduct your research. Pink Sheets won't furnish you with any information regarding the businesses you're exchanging with, and on the the chance that you simply choose a company you're increasing the risk and increasing likely that you'll be unable to recover the entire amount of your money.

The Classifications System

As mentioned previously in the previous paragraph, as mentioned previously, the Pink Sheets framework has an arrangement for each of the exchange companies using it. This allows you to determine if a company is considered to be high risk or safe , and you can decide on your decisions based on this. Some of the levels found in the framework of grouping include:

Trusted Tier

Within the confided-in level within the Pink Sheets, you will discover the international equally American businesses that are considered as trustworthy and friendly. The companies that come from other countries are on the global trade, but they could currently be included in this level of confided-in. The companies that are on this group have not yet met the criteria to be included part of the regular Stock Exchange, yet this usually happens due to some minor problems because it is the Stock Exchange is so exacting.

In spite of their inability to get on the Stock Exchange, these companies could not be listed on the Stock

Trade They had the option to submit a review for free. This list of times focuses on organizations that are American that meet the standards necessary to be a part of NASDAQ but they don't submit SEC reports, and therefore they'd be transferred onto Pink Sheets.

Transparent Tier

It is a stage at which organizations will submit SEC reports and , now it will also include those from Bulletin Boards for Over-the-Counter. They are extremely trusted businesses since you'll be able to access some of their financial reports as well as other information which is needed to be able to meet the requirements of the SEC. You have the choice to research the companies since it's available to you and could save a lot of confusion and hassle when choosing the penny stocks you want to invest in.

Distressed Tier

The organizations that fall under this category of Pink Sheets are ones that offer limited data for financial specialists to examine and, often, they are not adhering to the guidelines defined in Pink Sheets. They may not be able to provide new information to the SEC as they ought to but some will use OTC exposures. They're not bad to deal with, however at times you need to be aware to the fact that they're not transmitting accurate data and some have been unable to do so.

Dark Tier

This is the one you must be aware of because of the possibility that it could trigger a number of problems. The companies that fall under this particular category aren't putting for any information to be sent off the road. They don't have data recorded for or through or both the SEC as well as OTC. OTC Disclosure administration, and they aren't doing this over at least the past half-year, which makes it difficult for the financial professional to come up with any notion of what this Stock is doing. Some companies which fall into this category. also slipping with simpleness in the market, or do not have a market indicator.

Toxic Tier

As a financial expert or any other type of speculator as long in that regard it is best to stay clear of the poisonous levels. Companies that fall into this type of situation will usually rely on advertising methods that are not authentic like using methods that aren't working or sending out a huge amount of spam to provide examples. They may also include some organizations who are in the midst of massive corporate events that make them uncomfortable or may be subject to a suspension from the legislature. Sometime, these organizations won't have their own business responsibilities and are extremely risky for you to pay your cash to.

Analyzing the different levels in this framework can aid you in making a an informed decision in how to work with the Pink Sheets. You have the choice to compare these scores with any organization you choose to work with, and on the possibility that you choose the one with the highest well-known, it becomes more straightforward to earn great returns from ventures.

What to Do When Making Decisions on Pink Sheets

As we learn information about the Pink Sheets and their workings and function, it's time to decide the best way to exchange options. If you choose a penny stock which is listed on Pink Sheets, you will be restricted to data and an in-depth study on the part of most of companies. There are also a few problems that arise every now and then because of the fact that there's nothing but a single exchange that can be used to buy and sell the Stocks. This is the reason why it is recommended to start with an agent or vendor who are able to guide you through the process.

As a speculator, you must conduct a fundamental study of any business you are required to invest resources into regardless of whether or not delivering the information to you. You could look at the different organizations as well as their past history. you could try to determine whether there are any hidden gems that other people will not pick in the present, but that will benefit the Stock in the future. By conducting a thorough examination you'll have the ability to restrict the choices you have to take advantage of.

Utilizing Pink Sheets can be one way to get started on Penny Stocks, however you must be careful. Certain companies are exceptional and offer the information needed to select from; large numbers of them are trying to make it to the Stock Exchange, yet for an explanation of some kind or another the fact that they're not there yet, and they are completely safe options to consider. But, there are also businesses who are on the Pink Sheets that won't give any information and some are fake, and you must be wary of the companies you invest funds into to ensure that your portfolio is solid and growing.

Investing in OTC Bulletin Boards

Another option you could choose to make for those Penny Stocks is the Over-the-Counter Bulletin Boards, or the OTC Boards. This is in all likelihood in the United States, is worked by the Financial Industry Regulatory Authority and it is home to a significant number of Stocks and security measures that aren't available at the NASDAQ or other Stock Exchanges. It is recommended to work with vendors and merchants in order to buy as well as sell your Penny Stocks as this isn't an electronic process, and it is generally safe to use.

This kind of Penny Stock is typically considered to be more secure due to the fact that they need to transfer money-related data as well as to be simple. The focus is more on this and often the companies who are listed on this stock are listed because they failed to meet a small requirement to be included in the market. The majority of the companies listed in this announcement must report their information to the SEC However, they aren't required to report all the information they would do on the Stock Exchange and they can save our information in their market's upper case, providing value, administrative and even some.

They are usually regarded as being more secure because of the way these businesses have to submit information and submit reports to the SEC in contrast to the companies that are listed on their Pink Sheets could do this disclosure, but weren't required to. Many apprentices who are working in Penny Stocks will decide to opt for this option because it allows them to become familiar with the business they'll need to invest money in and enables them to select a smart investment for themselves.

The OTC Bulletin Boards as well as the Pink Sheets can be extraordinary submissions that can help you to find the penny stock which you must invest your money into. Certain options could be risky however, as a good gambler, it's on you to take a step and conduct a thorough investigation to uncover this information. There are risky ventures no matter the place you are located, on or off the stock market or in other forms of contributions, but you must choose the strategy that is most effectively for you and has the appropriate hazard-to-remuneration proportion that you're comfortable with. Both strategies for exchanging come with their own frameworks to help you decide on the right options. Also, on the possibility that you work as an agent, or seller, it is essential to receive the support you require to make the best option.

Chapter 2: What are Penny Stocks?

This book is on trading penny stocks, also known as "penny stocking". Penny stocking is the practice to trade penny stocks. Penny stocks are stock that trades for an extremely low cost and market capitalization in comparison to other stocks. They typically trade in a different market than the main exchanges. They are usually considered highly risky and speculative. There are a variety of reasons for penny stocks to be considered as more risky than other kinds of securities. The most important reason is due to their lack liquidity, huge bid-ask spreads smaller capitalization, as well as limited follow-up and the lack of disclosure. The majority of penny stocks trade on the open market through OTCBB and pink sheets. OTCBB as well as pink sheets.

What are the reasons to invest in this stock instead of larger known ones? It's not about investing in large, established businesses for long durations of time. This is not the purpose of penny stocking. about. The penny stocking market is all about instants rather than long periods of waiting and determination. It's an "get into and out quick" kind of trading.

Penny stocking is all about riding the speculative waves. What is this referring to? Penny stocks are intended to be purchased and sold quickly. It's about buying large quantities of stock and then selling them as fast as their value increases and generating a significant gains in the space of days or hours.

The most crucial aspect to do to make profits from this method is understanding the "waves". To be an excellent investment shopper, the most crucial thing is to understand that penny stocking is an activity, not an investment that lasts for the rest of your life. An excellent poker player can earn millions of dollars, and penny stockers are more similar to gamblers than an investor.

It is crucial not to overlook the preceding paragraph. It can make an important difference in cashing in and successfully cashing out as opposed to. throwing away your cash. It is now time to understand the game. In my time as a penny stock holder, I have experienced great results as well as a few moments of failure. The failed investments I have observed share a commonality Around 90% of the people who make losses through penny stocking say that they didn't think they understood of the "rules" in the sport. They plunged into the ocean and did not take the time to understand the ocean's waves.

Everyone has been a victim of losses at times in a particular investment however, in the end, what matters is that the balance is drawn up in green. Everybody asks me if it's actually possible to earn an income from trading penny stocks. The solution can be "Yes". However, it is crucial to learn and implement the principles of market. It is only the way you can transform the $5000 amount into hundreds of thousands or more. I'll then share my ideas to help you create an effective strategy for market entry within this guide. A lot of people believe that it's a matter of destiny, but it's not the fate that can make you money. It's experience, skill and experience to give you the extravagant lifestyle you've always dreamed of.

It is true that there are a few transactions that can earn your hundreds of thousands in money. it is essential to be aware of that since many investors miss the chance to earn up to 500% in their investments with the hope to make even more profits at time the day only to be met with the dismal disappointment of their stocks losing value in just a couple of hours.It is crucial to realize that many transactions won't yield any profit over one thousand dollars, however, it is the continuous play and concentration that can allow an ongoing flow of money to your bank account. One of the most important guidelines I'd like you to know is the fact that penny stocks could earn lots of cash however, there are a few things to take into consideration.

Many people learn their lessons the worst manner possible which means they lose a significant amount of money. The primary goal in this guide is to avoid your life from that fate. After reading this book you might find that you are wondering if these are risky investments. And I don't mean to take you to battle without warning: they are. They're dangerous.In reality, everything is risky including a bus ride to nightclubbing, therefore it is crucial to take the enough time to study the penny stocks so that you can understand their risks, and to look beyond your eyes when it comes time to convert your savings into stocks.

Penny stocks offer the possibility of both risk and reward but not in the same way as other kinds of investments. What can I do to reduce the risk? There is only one way: Reading. An attentive and consistent reading of the media on economics, and dedication to a thorough understanding of your investment. That is the sole method to minimize the risks and also boosting your profit by avoiding the commissions imposed by stockbrokers and you will not rely on their honesty or knowledge that is an crucial aspect when it comes to investing.

In this article, you will meet an axiom which have been the basis of my success: I rely on my expertise and understanding when I pay attention to it, I could possess the same or greater understanding than the average stockbroker. For trading this kind of stock, you do not require a stockbroker license and, as I've said before, there is no have to search for any of them. Penny stocks are a unique investment which do not need the type of know-how and experience that comes from an experienced stockbroker. Your own understanding of the stock, the company and the situation of the sector(s) that is affecting the market are far more crucial. This gives everyone the chance to become a successful investment when they spend the time to understand. Very few are those who earn a living out of penny stocking, and less are the companies who dedicate themselves to the practice.

In this guide , I'll expose the plan for what I believe will be many years of success in penny-stocking.

Chapter 3: Steps to Start Using Penny Stocks

It's time to put your feet in the water. This chapter will cover everything you'll need to know in order before you can begin trading. Once you've started your journey into trading, think realistically regarding the time you'll be able to devote to studying and monitoring prices of stocks. It is a long-term shift in your financial situation. I would like you to begin immediately but I'd like to ensure that you're in the proper approach. Refer to Chapter 2 to learn about strategies that traders employ to earn a profit. Also, make sure you've taken the time to absorb the information before making an initial trade.

Get Started Looking At The Exchanges

Penny stocks trade on three exchanges. They range from the well-known NASDAQ up to Pink Sheets, which has practically no requirements to list a business. The final exchange and one that you typically use is the OTCBB also known as the over-the-counter Bulletin Board exchange. The OTCBB has a large collection from penny stock that are in line with the minimum requirements, but they are priced appropriately at lower than one-dollar. The NASDAQ will not permit stocks to be listed until they are valued at one-dollar or greater. Additionally the market capitalization reviews have more depth than those of the others, which makes the NASDAQ a great option for investors who want to keep stocks in reserve for a period of time. period of.

You should examine each individual exchange. They are directly competing with each with each other, and are continually increasing the range of services they provide. Although they are not perfect, the Pink Sheets are still not highly reputable however, they are working to raise their profile with investors and with the world as a as a whole. Recently, they introduced the OTCQX - - a different part within the Pink Sheets that offers premium stocks that are better examined. The stocks have to satisfy certain minimums and be divided into three distinct categories based on the stock's worth. Learn about each exchange's operating hours and, perhaps, a more about their history. The OTCQX has won the hearts of the majority of investors as well. Pink Sheets is seeing more activity than it has seen in many years, however their reputation remains an issue. Due to their past of poor testing and lack of standards, there's nothing an exchange of this quality could do to alter my belief that the stocks they offer are properly evaluated. It doesn't mean you won't earn money from these Pink Sheets - they are in fact a very lucrative income source for a lot of investors, however, you'll be interested in knowing their history and be aware of what you're purchasing and why you're purchasing it.

After looking over the exchanges and figuring out the information that are available on each exchange the exchanges, it is important to study the historical data for each exchange to discover the case histories of stocks under certain conditions. Penny stocks differ from other exchanges because of their minimums, yet they are still governed by the fundamental economic rules and share interactions within financial markets. This means that in rough times, cosmetics businesses, liquor distributors and producers of small-scale consumable items perform well, while the boom time companies have larger quantities of products do better. Get familiar with these trends by studying the sector interests you. They do not have to be clearly defined and instead, just follow your passions. If you're interested in a passion for fashion , take a take a look at a variety of clothing firms and observe what they've been up to in during the past few months, or during times of slowdown or boom in the market. There is a lot to learn through thisprocess, and you'll begin to comprehend your industry a small amount better by each company you investigate. You are free to investigate businesses that do not fall within an area that you are knowledgeable about and be aware of what this industry is doing to get an idea of the general trends in the coming years.

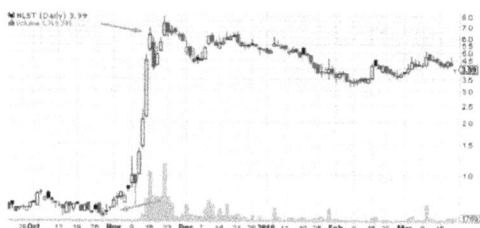

Then, consider the performance of different sectors across the various exchanges. It is likely that, while general market trends can be an excellent predictor of the how a specific sector will perform exchanges can also determine the volatility of certain areas. For example, companies in the tech sector that are listed on the Pink Sheets tend to be more volatile than companies that are listed at the NASDAQ. This could be an incentive to trade on those Pink Sheets, but if you're looking to implement an investment strategy that involves holding and buying then it is better to purchase from the NASDAQ. They won't rise like the ones shown in the Pink Sheets, but for long-term investment, they are much more likely to be able to weather markets and stand a higher chances of making waves and gaining world-wide recognition. You've studied the various kinds of theories of trading and aware of which one is appealing to you. Remember this as you examine the different exchanges, focusing on the exchange that is most suitable to suit your particular strategy and your particular area of interest.

Start with a Zero Investment

Once you've looked through the exchanges and become familiar with their workings and how they work, you're ready to begin investing. The next step will be to choose out a few companies and then "buy the stock at a price you are able to pay for right now. Make this a priority, but don't buy anything. Instead, note down what you'd like to purchase, the number of shares and the date of purchase. It is important to buy shares in amounts that you are able to manage because this is your practice session and you're practicing for the real-world conditions. In each transaction it is recommended to take a deduction of five or ten dollars from the purchase and sell as this is a resemblance to the price of the brokerage's commission. When you purchase stock, you should sell when you've earned profits, or your losses are too high to bear. It is tempting to lie on your journal, but write down the date you sold your stock at a specific time, but you did not intend on selling, other than with hindsight. Keep your word to yourself because lying only does you disservice.

As well as noting the stocks you purchase and selling, you should keep track of the reasons behind buying an investment and the amount of hours it took you to make your conclusion. This is an excellent time to consider how much time you invest. This will allow you to calculate the amount you earn per hour and let you know whether you should concentrate on a different approach. Keep track of your losses total and the profits you earn - these figures are the amount you can realistically expect that you can earn each week.

If you execute some amazing trades during this period, don't be disappointed that you will not receive any cash. Instead , focus on the things you did well with the trade. There are a set of conditions on every trade that can bring you profits. Follow what is working for you, and you will remain constant. In my case, it's the option to trade on technology stocks. It's an area I've got some knowledge in however, even though I usually do my trading based on the price It's helpful to be able to find out the background of a company and know what kind of product or service they're selling. I also know about competition and the possibility of their success. Choose your field and get into it; you'll need to find a good location when you begin making money.

How to Choose A Broker

Picking a broker to trade penny stocks is simple. You only need to decide which broker is best suited to your requirements. Brokers vary in their charges and services offered as well as the quality of tools offered and minimum purchase orders. There's a lot of information and I'll cover each of them and then one of the things every broker you pick should be able to access several exchanges. With online brokers, you will have access to NASDAQ or OTCBB. I don't recommend you only trade on the NASDAQ however, be aware that brokers who specialize in these exchanges usually offer higher rates and more requirements for purchase orders. At present, my preferred brokerage is LowTraders.com. Be aware that I'll change when I find an alternative brokerage. Likewise, you should also be prepared to change if you discover better prices.

The primary distinction between penny stock brokers is the amount they charge to make a single transaction. In the case of the amount you are looking to invest your margins at first could be very low. It is important be thinking about taking a minimum of ten dollars for each deal to make up the purchase and sell cost for the broker. 5 dollars are the cheapest I've ever experienced, but rates will become more expensive when you start to explore more luxurious services. Brokerage firms which specialize in Dow Jones and NASDAQ might provide trading with low latency, or promise that their transactions get through quicker than anyone else. Beware of the rumors that these transactions are executed with the same speed regardless of which broker you choose to use. The variation in time, if it is there, will be measured in milliseconds. For certain traders, this is significant, but it isn't in penny stock. Make sure you choose an online broker that offers five dollars in free transactions for each trade, and don't pay attention to the details of high-speed trading.

It is also important to be aware of the type of services they offer. Certain brokerage companies offer full-service, while others just manage your trades. Firms that offer clients who are full service will charge higher than 5 dollars for each trade however, take note that they provide financial advice to their customers, and are usually accessible for one-on-one contact. When it comes to penny stock, these kinds of companies aren't very efficient. Companies trading at such tiny value per share are typically not in the sights of companies offering these services. They may offer assistance to but in reality, they'll be of no assistance.

A differentiator among brokers lies in the tools they provide. These tools are generally included in the bells and whistles provided by brokerage companies. They'll provide tools for monitoring the price of stocks, and send emails to your inbox whenever a certain price has been reached and more. It's difficult to recommend an investment firm using their own set of tools, as a variety of top-quality free tools are available. Based on the way you think about trading, you may want to invest a bit more if you think the tool you choose will prove to be a great asset but do a few Google searches will allow you to discover something that works for you as effectively. Personally, I use OTC market tools. OTC marketplace tools. They're not the most user-friendly initially but they're not too difficult to use that it's worth paying more money to get something that's simpler and more user-friendly.

The final thing you need to take note of is the minimum purchase order. In addition to the fee for each trade in stock it is also necessary to purchase a certain number of shares. Certain brokerage firms require the exact quantity of shares to be their minimal requirement, however in the world of penny stocks, these minimums are usually the price of the entire purchase. They will differ between brokers, however, it is recommended that each transaction is at least $30. While this may be an issue, the value you get per share is not high enough that you'll want to place purchases of at least the size of this. I've already mentioned this however, I currently use LowTraders.com for my majority of purchases. It is still advisable to explore other options since new competitions appear on the market every day. Once you are accustomed in a particular broker you'll need to often look into alternatives to determine whether a different broker might serve you better.

Try Different Theories

Now you should be ready to invest, and I hope you've had enough experience with your journals that you are comfortable with investing in penny stocks. The method you choose to apply to trading is a reflection of your interest, time as well as your financial resources. It is recommended to try some trades using every method regardless of your interest level with any particular approach. This is because I've discovered that individuals have inherent abilities in investing, and their abilities are different from what they believed their capabilities were. When I was trading with traditional exchanges I concentrated on long-term trading It was my specialty and I was adept in choosing winners. I employed a method that involved investing in about 10 companies, and in six months, usually one of them had paid off in a way that covered my losses on companies that failed to perform. I tried this approach using penny stocks, but it did not perform. I believe that I'm naturally skilled in long-term trades, however this skill isn't suited into penny stock. The point is keeping your eyes open and try different methods. I didn't think that trading swings would be an ideal choice for me, however, now this is by far the only kind of trading I engage in.

Chapter 4: Starting with Penny Stocks

After you have mastered the various terms, let's get to know the basics of trading. Here are a few things you'll require to be able to trade penny stocks with success.

A computer

The first thing you need is an computer. Although you may consider purchasing an laptop, it would be better to use desktops. Desktops give you the feeling of an office and you don't need to fret about carrying the laptop everywhere. You can create an office you can block others from entering the space.

Desktop computers are generally more secure because you can't carry it to public areas. If you are looking to trade while on the move There are a lot of applications that allow you to access the information stored on your desktop computer So you don't have to be concerned about moving around. However, you must ensure that you protect your password on your devices you use to trade stocks.

Connection that is reliable

This is an important point that I cannot emphasize enough. Technology has changed the way stock trading is conducted over the past couple of decades , and trading on the internet has become the only method for trading in stocks. It is impossible to trade stocks without access to an Internet connection. Actually, it is impossible to trade with penny stock if do not have a reliable and speedy Internet connection. You've probably guessed that this market is highly unpredictable and is likely to fluctuate dramatically. If you are unable to find something, you'll need to accept a loss. Every second is important when it comes to the penny market. Therefore, it is recommended to have a speedy as well as solid Internet connection.

In the end purchasing and selling stocks is like going to an auction. It demands your full attention and attention, otherwise an opportunity might be missed. In addition to an efficient Internet as well, it's good to have a power backup plan. If you lost power the entire work you had been doing might be lost if it wasn't backup your data in time, and you might miss many fantastic opportunities. Installing a backup battery on your computer's desktop is an inexpensive and straightforward method to avoid this issue.

Account for trading

Even though you are required to purchase as well as sell penny stocks on the market however, you may still require an account for trading on penny stocks. In this case, you need to sign up for an account at the trading company. The firm must be reliable, and you may verify their credentials prior to making an account them. Remember that the costs vary widely between brokers. There are typically slight differences in trading firms' policies be sure to study the details before you pick the one you prefer.

The process to open an account is typically quite simple It is as simple as having to complete the required information and then provide them with the necessary documents in order to satisfy the legal obligations. After your account is set up operating, then you are able to start trading.

Broker

It is the next thing to do: hire an agent who can help you navigate the right steps. This is an essential step if you're brand novice to penny stocks but don't know how to approach things. A broker has access to all of the necessary information and is in a position to help you. You must find a reputable broker make sure to conduct an investigation into their background if it is possible. The broker should have previous experience and have worked in penny stock. They should be a licensed broker with the proper accreditation. The process of contacting a financial institution to find a broker most likely the best thing to do as you'll be able to find the perfect one.

Budget

The next step is to decide on the budget. You must set an amount that will allow you to invest the appropriate amount of money in the market. It is important to consider an amount that is enough to begin investing in penny stock. Don't make a huge budget. The penny stocks are those with prices that are priced between $5 and $10, so that you don't require a huge budget to invest in it. It is possible to add cash as and when feel it is appropriate to do so.

This step is crucial because the last thing you want is to be into a bind. Establish a daily limit for the amount you are able to invest and adhere to the limit. It is not advisable to spend more than your budget, unless there is a specific situation. If you're married setting a budget can demonstrate to your spouse that you're accountable. If you are planning to overspend your budget be sure to discuss it to your broker, or advisor.

Research

It is essential to conduct thorough studies on the subject so that you can invest intelligently. Your research should be focused on understanding the fundamentals regarding penny stocks and what they are able to offer you and how they can help your portfolio, and how safe they are, and so on. Beyond just reading about financial news, you should also look at general news in the national context. Recent events can affect the market in the same way as the background of a company , or the situation in local politics. In other words, you'll have to be an educated person who is up to date with the current trends to become a successful trading penny stocks.

After you have completed the initial research, it is now time to shift to analyzing the top investments to make. There are a few stocks that within the penny range will be a wise investment, and you should choose the ones that you believe to be doing well in the present. After you have narrowed down a few that you like, you can choose the most profitable among them.

Be sure to seek advice, particularly when you are choosing the first stocks. Once you've gained some experience you could also feel more at ease purchasing or selling stocks without consulting anyone who is not the first person to consult, but this should be an case, not the standard. The experience of someone else can assist you in the same way as, if not more than your own experience.

Message boards

Another thing worth exploring is message boards. These are forums where users post messages on excellent stocks they want to recommend. These suggestions are designed to help investors make choice on what stocks to invest in as well as which to stay clear of. It is possible to determine the trending stocks and which ones aren't doing well. There will be users and bashers within the community. They will be promoting an excellent stock by asking buyers to buy it while the latter will slam an investment, which will lower its value. It is important to look over these boards in order to determine who is actually recommending excellent stocks and how they're doing on the stock market.

Be sure to be participating in various types of message boards to gain a comprehensive perspective on the marketplace. Chat rooms on Facebook, online chat groups as well as the local communities are all great alternatives, to mention just some.

Journal

It is essential to keep a journal to record every experience you have had in the market for stocks. Keep a log of your investments , from the stocks you choose from the investment amount to any other information you believe should be documented. You can opt for an electronic or physical journal for your journal. It is essential to dedicate your time to writing your entries so that you can keep the same journal. Reviewing your journal will allow you to avoid mistakes and keep you on the right track.

You must keep track of each when you buy or sell stocks. Make sure you organize your journals so that it is easy to read. Separating it into sections for all kinds of investments including penny stocks and the precious metals is an excellent way to begin. In addition, note your top stocks and the ones you are performing well. When you look through your journal, you'll probably be able to identify any patterns that are emerging in your success when compared to your losses. This will assist in identifying the things you need to avoid.

There are a variety of aspects to consider in the event that you want to start trading small-sized stocks.Armed by these instruments, you're well-prepared to dive into the action. The next step is to explore what makes these penny stocks work.

Chapter 5: Crucial Factors That Will Make You Successful

The success of investing with penny stocks can be similar to playing poker. It is not simply by chance. For success you must invest time, energy, and do a thorough study on the matter. If only people would slow down and think about how little effort they invest into their investing, they'd not be able to understand why they constantly have to lose money. While there isn't a assurance of making money however, there are some strategies you can take to increase the chances of being successful. These are the practices that successful traders perform every day. You should incorporate these into your routine also.

Do your research

When conducting research, you should not only look at the stocks you are looking to buy. They're simply a by-product. You must conduct an extensive research. You should investigate the company that you are purchasing the stock. You must research and study the way in which the company performs with its rivals. What is its position in the marketplace? Does it get the approval of the market it is targeting? The more you understand about a company's business, the higher your odds for investing in best profit-making stocks. If you're looking to make a serious effort with penny stocks, thorough research is something is not to be missed.

Examine the patterns

Take note of and study the graphs that demonstrate the performance of specific penny stocks. Don't limit yourself to the current performance. Instead, you should study their price patterns over the long term. Even if a particular stock does well, don't make a decision to invest immediately. It is also important to evaluate the performance of the stock against its peers. The performance of any business is always dependent on its competitors. is based upon the success of competition. So, remain open-minded and conduct research on the various businesses.

Many investors at first focus so heavily on trends. Although they can provide certain patterns that could aid you in making an informed decision, these patterns can also be difficult to discern. Be aware that trends can change even when you don't anticipate it. There are many elements that affect the worth in penny stocks. While it is advised to be aware of patterns as you observe them, it's ideal to be aware of the situation.

Stay up to date with the most recent information

Stay up-to-date with the most recent news and be aware of the factors which affect the risk in penny stock. When you know what events happen around you, you'll be able to be aware of the penny stocks worthy of investing in. But, you should not follow the same path as others who are distracted by the information. Keep in mind that while being aware of news events can be helpful but what is most important is the actual numbers or the values which are displayed in the penny market.

Only invest money that you are able to afford losing

It is a well-known gambler's advice. While making investments in penny stocks isn't like placing bets on the roulette wheel, it is real that some risks are present. There is no assurance that you'll come out with a return. Therefore, you should not make use of your funds to pay electricity bills or other expenses for your household. If a supposedly "expert" advises you to invest in a specific stock that will double or triple your investment in the span of a week however, even when your own research supports this possibility, do not invest with money you are able to afford losing. In the end, even the most reputable penny stock investors make poor investment choices at times.

Set a limit

Because of the extreme rate of change of penny stock, don't keep a streak going for too long. There is no assurance that a company that has recently tripled in value will perform well on the market. If the price falls it is likely that you will go through the loss of any value you've enjoyed. So, you should set a target and remain conscientious enough to make a cash withdrawal (sell) when you reach your goal value. It might not be advisable to cash out immediately in the event of a situation that suggests that the value of penny stocks is still rising. However, while you should be wary but you must be on the lookout for lucrative opportunities. You must also do some thorough research to determine if holding on to a specific stock is still a wise choice.

In the event that, instead of experiencing a constant rise in value and you experience a constant reduction in value then you must establish a reasonable limit the extent to which you prepared to commit to a stock that is losing value. Don't be afraid to make rash investments. There are risks involved in dealing when investing in penny stocks. It is important to reduce your losses so that you will make a positive net profit at the final.

Seek out patterns

Penny stocks are extremely speculated. There are many variables that impact their prices that are beyond your control. The way they fluctuate in price is near to being random. But, even the results derived from random generators can create patterns. While these patterns aren't continuously created, if one can recognize them once they occur, there's more chance to make an investment that is sound.

Make your own decisions

While it's good to get experts, particularly when you're just starting to trade penny stocks, experienced traders will inform you that it's recommended to develop your own plan of action and understand of the market for penny stocks. Experts become experts when they are able to think independently. They make informed investment decisionsthat are backed by their studies and research. However, the most experienced investors make mistakes from time-to-time as is the norm particularly if you are trading or investing in penny stock. After all, development does not happen overnight. It's a continuous process that will never stop.

Another reason to decide for yourself is that there are a lot of scams and schemes that are available. They can make you believe that penny stocks are worthwhile to invest in. They will persuade you to invest your money only to gain from the deal. This is typical when you're caught in an 'pump and dump' scheme. Be cautious and take every information with the grain of salt. Be open to learning however, you must be able to make a decision yourself.

Never chase after your losses

Accept losses as they happen. If you are truly involved trading penny shares, the losses are a part of business. However, you shouldn't chase the losses. It's like keeping the price of a stock that decreases every day. Instead, concentrate on your top-performing stocks. Make sure you learn from each error and be sure not to be disappointed when you decide to sell a stock that is losing money. Learn to be gentle with yourself, particularly after you have made a poor investment choice. Take your losses as part of the learning curve for about penny stock investing.

Be calm and be aware.

No matter if you're the owner of a stock that is losing value or one that has an ever increasing value, be calm and remain focused. One of the most frequent mistakes made by investors is to allow their emotions to dictate their actions. In most cases, this doesn't perform well in the business of penny stocks. Keep in mind that when dealing when dealing with penny stocks it is essential to be able to work with numbers and real facts. Do not make any decisions while under stress.

Avoid being greedy

Any rise in value you experience could soon be a negative. The high volatility is part of the nature of penny stocks. Therefore, you should not be overly frenzied. Cash out and sell your earnings before you're all out. Greed is among the main reasons that investors are unable to recover their investment.

Create a strategy and adhere to it

Before you buy an amount of money You must know what you're planning to accomplish with the stock. It is important to follow this plan and follow it. The most frequent mistake that investors make is when they have a solid strategy, but because of an unanticipated drop in the value of their stocks, they get scared and do not adhere to their strategy. This is a bad practice in two ways. First, since they do not follow through with their plan, they don't be able to tell if their strategy working or not. In the second, often, making changes to a plan causes you to use a less effective strategy.

Of obviously, you do not have to adhere to your plan when circumstances indicate that it could result in the loss of your money. If you are forced to alter your plan because of an imminent loss, it is imperative to come up with a new alternative. That means, the next plan should be well thought of and provide a solid plan.

Thus, you must stick the plan. If there's an important change in the circumstances, in which a change of plan is an ideal option to avoid any loss that is imminent, be certain that your contingency plan is at least as secure as the initial one. Meaning, do not rush it. Make the time to analyze and study your next step.

Do not invest in penny stocks with an abundance of

Another issue with penny stocks is that, even if the value of your stock dramatically increases, there's no way to convert your gains into money when no one is willing to purchase your stocks. Thus, experts typically suggest that you invest in stocks from companies that have an adequate number of transactions every day. The best number depends on particularly when taking into consideration the reliability and reputation of a company. Based on the "expert," companies that are trading at least 100,000 shares every day are highly recommended.

Make sure you are pumping your stocks

You could put your money into low-cost penny stocks, then use certain marketing techniques to boost the value of their stock, and then sell them to make an income. It's like the pump and dump method. A lot of people make money doing this If you don't like pumping your own stock it is a great method to earn cash, particularly if are someone with a convincing skills. An effective method to do this is to create an online presence or blog that projects the image of an experienced trader in penny stock. In addition you could also provide your penny stocks for auction. If you decide to do this it is crucial to keep a low profile when it comes to making money from it; otherwise, people will view you as another fraudster. Be sure to make your blog or website as informative as possible to ensure that your visitors are able to learn something new every when they visit your website. Through sharing helpful information and information, you will earn confidence from your visitors.

Concentrate on startups

This requires more study, but it can greatly increase your odds of making money. You must identify and analyze the various startups which issue penny stocks. Examine how they do on the market and how they compare against their competition and how much profits they generate. Be aware that startups aren't perfect and have a lot of room for improvement. As they grow, prices of their stock also rise. Thus, if you find a company in the early stages that is actually growing and it is evident that it will continue to be profitable over the long term and will continue to grow, it is beneficial for you to buy its penny stocks and make the most of its hard work and its success.

The laziest method

It isn't a suggested method, but you may be interested in giving it a try to have fun or when you're too lazy to put in the effort. Simply look to find penny-stocks that you think are getting attention and being popular before making an investment. If the price goes up by at least

5% to 10 percent, place a buy order. One way to stay informed about the penny stocks that are growing in popularity is to join various social media groups that focus on penny stocks, as being a part of online forums.

Keep a journal

It is essential to not forget to record in your diary every investment decision you make. Journals can help you to think outside of the box and take better decisions. Be assured that you don't need to be an expert writer. It is enough be truthful and capable of writing down and keep a record of as many times as you can. In the ideal scenario, you will keep your journal updated regularly or even daily. It is also possible to write in your journal your thoughts on specific investments you make. While keeping a journal might take some effort on your part however, you'll appreciate it, particularly when you are analyzing your strategies.

Receive the latest information quickly.

While they are high-risk Penny stocks have an underlying pattern that is: their prices remain constant and fluctuate regardless of whether the increase or decrease in value is due to legitimate motives or otherwise. They are very sensitive and are unable to be insulated from the reality of having an extreme volatility.

One of the best ways to earn money is to know the most recent news regarding penny stocks. It is essential to be aware immediately when certain stocks are likely to become popular. It is better to know the news before it is published. It is also important to be sure you know that penny stock in question are actively promoted. If this is the case it is essential to make an investment in these stocks immediately, as the value of these stocks will rise. However, you must be prepared to sell them in an hour. The value of them will increase because of the increasing interest and popularity. It is advised not to get too greedy and to sell them when you have at least five percent rise. It is a smart method to earn a steady income from penny stocks. It is also possible to use this strategy to determine if someone who knows that he is involved in the pump and dump scam. Of course, it is possible to try to make more profit in the absence of selling stock immediately however the amount of risk higher. Additionally, you don't have to sell all of the stocks in one go. If you feel that selling your stock would be an unwise decision, then you could just sell 40-60 percent of your investment and let the remaining stocks enjoy the highs. However, you must be prepared to pay out at some moment.

Pause for a moment

It's not unusual to witness investors become obsessed with the trading of penny stock. In the end, this type of business is similar to gambling. But, don't be able to forget to break. You can forget about penny stocks for a while. Just enjoy your the moment and spend time with your family. It is essential to get enough sleep for achieving more mental focus.

Have fun!

As with everything else in life, it's always more enjoyable when you're having enjoyable. Therefore, have fun playing having fun with the "game" and don't take it too seriously. No matter if you make a money or not, just take the time to enjoy yourself. Enjoy any money you earn and try to remain relaxed and calm whenever you suffer loss.

Be patient

While you are able to make several trades within a 24 hour time frame, it's better to employ strategies that will last for a couple of days. You must be patient and watch for the perfect moment to take advantage of the volatility that penny stocks can be leveraged in your favor. However, don't wait for too long, or else the trend could alter and cause a loss of value of your penny stocks.

Make use of the volatility's high to your advantage

On the other the other hand, many people claim that the extreme level of volatility in penny stocks makes them a bad investment for investing in. However it is the presence of such high volatility which could allow you to earn lots of cash by trading and investing in penny stocks. It is all you need to do is to find the best penny stocks, allow some space (so they of the stock can rise) before making a the decision to either sell or buy.

It doesn't matter if you're a novice or an experienced trader. With the advent of Internet has allowed everyone to gain access to a wealth of information, the sole thing that differentiates an individual who is a novice from those who have a good understanding of that the way the penny stock market operates is the level of knowledge. Only that you actually apply what you've learned that you can be more successful as an investor. Be prepared to make mistakes and make significant profit.

Chapter 6: Habits of Learning from Others People

As you fight to climb that mountain, others have made it to their summits and they are headed down. A few people might offer suggestions regarding how to complete your climb, too. It's advantageous to accept these suggestions and assistance. Similar to trading stocks, you will be able to meet others who have gone through the same thing and come back as a winner. It is advantageous for your success too. Spend the time to get familiar with their strategies and methods. Read about the personal stories of successful traders you have heard of. If you can learn from them. Some pay these people to be their coaches. This is a significant investment. What they possess is not only the technical aspects of trading but also actual experience and the innate insight. You can also benefit by observing their failures. It is not necessary to learn by doing it the hard way. They already did it. You may be able to avoid making similar mistakes if you took your time and learn from their mistakes. The need for professional assistance is not an indication of vulnerability. Professionals can assist you learn more about stock trading and quicker.

Warren Buffet has much to discuss the stock market as well as trading in stocks. Learn from Warren Buffet. His billion-dollar assets today show that his strategies are effective. There is no need to outdo Warren Buffet and discover a more efficient method. It is possible to begin becoming successful by being humble and admitting that someone is superior to you. They've been through this. Learn from their experiences. According to the saying there is no have inventing the wheel. To sum up this idea we'll end with Warren's most famous quotes "In this business world, your rearview mirror is always more clear as the windscreen". This means that your past can be a source of inspiration than the present are facing.

The known and tested. It was successful for them. It is a good option for you. Learn from these experts. Here are some Warren's advice for investors.

Don't borrow money to invest. This is the quickest method to get broke. Make sure you take care of yourself first and foremost in all of your earnings. This means you put aside funds (suggestion is 20 percent) which you can then put aside later to invest.

Make investments in companies you trust and are not afraid being forced to deal with even in the event where it is the case that the Stock Exchange would be closed for the following year. So, it would not be a major cost for your.

The stock market doesn't have any feelings for you, so it is not appropriate to have feelings about them either. Avoid being emotionally involved with the stock market. Don't let the stock market influence your feelings.

Make it clear that you will be prosperous and wealthy. Positive thinking is crucial.

Warren was never doubtful that he could make a fortune and he did.

Spend less than what you earn. Warren is famous for his practicality and lived a little extravagantly, even though he was able to afford it. A person's standard of life for an average person is drastically altered with even the slightest increase in money. Keep a low-stress lifestyle.

Will Smith, the famous actor, was adamant that many people are spending money has not yet been earned (everything comes from credit). This is the reason that a lot of people in debt.

There are many other outstanding people and women worthy of a model. Their lives can inspire us to live a better lives to be more enjoyable. Use those. Learn from the experts.

Chapter 7: What to Select Winners In the Penny Stocks Arena

To allow you investors to gain an understanding regarding the future of your penny stock investment It is important to be aware of the stock's past. As the well-worn and reliable cliché is that history repeats itself. If you continue to move forward without taking time to reflect could result in you make the exact same errors other investors have repeated many times. In general, investors claim that penny stocks is simply different scenarios that repeatedly unfold time and repeatedly over and over again, generation after generation. Certain investors are under assumption that the old economic regulations will not be able to be applicable to new economy stocks however, regardless of what your personal opinion on this matter, it is a fact that studying the past is a sure way to prepare that a better future is possible. What are the steps to choose an investment that is profitable? In this guide, everything starts with the research you conduct.

How to find a PENSY STOCK BEFORE IT SPELLS

It's vital for penny stock traders to be able to recognize when a stock is going through a spike. Of course, there's no certainty that can let you know exactly what every stock is performing in every circumstance - this is the market for stocks and all that - but there are some indicators can be used to determine when the spikes will happen. Here are some methods to identify penny stocks prior to when they will spike (number 1 is likely to sound very familiar):

Do your research! Truthfully one of the main reason why people don't succeed when it comes to trading penny stocks is because they don't know the extent of research needed to be conducted or that they're simply too lazy to invest the effort into. Many penny stock traders simply require someone to inform them of what they need to do. The main issue with this scenario is that the person instructing the trader about the right thing to do, is likely to give thousands of other traders to follow the exact same advice. This means that all these traders will have already jumped towards the potential opportunity , which means that all that's left are scraps. This will not be enough to earn profits and may result in the investor to suffer losses.

The question is how do we discover the latest big story before the mass media does it? The answer is of course, doing research. Check a stock's filings and disclosures. Find out if it has recent SEC announcements in the filings. It's possible to discover that an investment is poised to go up in value based on the information you discover.

Bet on the price movement of a stock. Many investors make the error of trying to determine when a surge is likely to occur by visiting the chat room they prefer to chat with other participants to find out what stocks they think might be moving, or to determine the height they believe the price of a particular stock will to reach. Some investors might purchase an alert from a professional kind who can inform them of the best time to purchase based on their predictions of spikes.

It's not to say that every chat room is bad. Investors have made a great deal of money from advice from friends they trust on certain chat rooms. In the end, however chat rooms are an opportunity to talk. You should instead place your bets on a stock's price action. The price action of a stock is the way it moves its chart which will provide you the most accurate information on any stock. The most up-to-date information on any website on the internet can't reveal when a stock could reach the top of its range or if it's exceeded its VWAP however, the movement of the chart of a particular stock definitely will.

Look for stocks with the potential for breakouts and have reached new heights. As a penny stock holder is it advisable to keep an eye on stocks that are in line with this trend. This is particularly true of stocks that are holding their early highs and are still rising throughout the day. However, you must take care however. If you see this scenario unfold on an afternoon on a Friday there's a huge chance of a brief squeeze to be worked through the end at this moment.

You can piggyback on an investment that has risen somewhat already. Of the four strategies this one is sure to require less time than the other three. Piggybacking is when investors discover a company that is already heading up , and is actually one of the fastest ways of identifying a company which is poised to go up. There are many research tools online which can assist investors in finding the information they need. All you need to do is use these tools. We hope that you'll apply these methods to your own situation and hope that they can help you realize how crucial it is to prepare properly and yes, conduct study before investing in any stock, whether penny or otherwise. A most penny-stock investors choose not to do the effort required to thoroughly study the SEC reports of a company they might consider investing in let alone try to determine what this information means so in relation to the price of the stock going up or down. This is why the majority of penny stock traders will eventually end up destroying their portfolios due to insufficient preparation and knowledge. There's no reason to risk ending up in the same situation. Although many people do not find the process of preparing and researching an enjoyable task but remember that this book isn't telling you how to become rich quickly or to enjoy the most enjoyable time you've ever experienced. The goal in this guide is to teach you how to succeed in trading penny stocks , by offering proven methods and guidelines of experienced investors, and for you to be successful to give you the financial freedom you want. What is it that you need to be successful when investing in penny stocks? It requires a lot of the effort, and really difficult work at times even. It requires a lot of determination.

The success of trading penny stocks will require that you, the investor commit the effort and time required to gain the benefits you're hoping to reap. Investors who don't spend the required energy and time will not achieve the goals that you, as a committed trader can achieve and will not have the chance to enjoy the financial freedom you'll be able to take advantage of - simply because they didn't do what is required to succeed. Although proper planning might not be fun but it is essential to be successful in making trades with penny stock.

The potential for payoffs in STOCK PENNY

Given the danger and work You may be asking what a potential investor who is in a good place would want to invest in penny stocks. This is due to the risk of volatility. Penny stocks are susceptible to extreme volatility and fluctuations. This is why many investors are enticed by the prospect of being lucky enough to get an investment that they believe is able to rise from $0.09 to $9 within two weeks. Although this isn't usual, it has occurred. If you browse through enough discussion boards with a focus on investing, then you'll surely find many success stories of investors who share their experiences of making an impressive amount of money by playing pennies.'

It's extremely uncommon to find companies that are able to be able to successfully navigate the leap from penny stock to a power stock. However, when you do come across these stocks, they pay dividends in a amazing manner. Because the numbers in the penny stock market are extremely volatile and fluctuate significantly, some well-prepared investors have experienced gains that exceeded 1,000% in just one week. But the true problem lies in being capable of identifying an investment that is profitable, and this chapter will help to help you do.

Chapter 8: Trading Penny Stocks

We've given you useful tools and advice to date in this book to help you establish your regular or weekly routine of trading. The idea of buying penny stocks is fantastic however, they'll be of no use financially in the event that you don't sell to maximize the ROI. Trading is as careful as choosing the stocks you wish to buy and all of it blends into a seamless process that involves investing and trading as machines. The penny stock market is one that you'll need to pay at all times. Although it isn't possible stay online 100% the time, it's essential to monitor your stocks at least once a day and create alerts to help you to identify stocks that have the potential to earn. The idea of investing into your future is typically something you do when you are doing your regular life with family, work, and routine. Putting the time to your trading will be crucial to ensure success.

We won't give you an easy step-by-step procedure of how you can physically sell your stock. Based on the brokerage company you've chosen as well as the information and tips we've provided to you, the entire procedure should be fairly easy to you. What do you need to pay attention to? are the elements you must keep in mind when you go through the procedure of trading. In this section we'll look at the most effective ways to trade penny stocks. A few of the points might seem repetitive, but it's an essential element of the whole procedure and must be considered throughout your investment plan. From studying your stocks to selling them precisely when you want to earn the best returns, let's take a some time to look over the top 10 most crucial strategies for successful trading and management of penny stocks.

One-Success Stories

Whatever you search for whenever you Google penny stocks, you're going to see millions of stories of people who have made a thousand dollars millions of dollars. A few of the stories will be published in articles while others will be absurd schemes that ask for you to purchase their book or have them guide you through similar things. Whatever it is, the strategy behind the story, do not believe it. Do not sign up for additional details, don't get sucked by flashy numbers and shorter time frames Don't be swayed by the hype you read. This guy could have five students that earned one million dollars within three years, but what does he not tell you is that the fact that he has hundreds of thousands of students.

As with numerous other aspects of life there's no secret formula that can take you from the ashes to the riches in just thirty days. The best thing to do is start with the grind, stick to the rules, apply the best practices and be focused on your objectives. It's great when you are able to sell your first stock to earn the best possible price, however, don't let the satisfaction. Instead, make use of it to determine what went right and what went wrong, and then tweak your methods to ensure that the next smart purchase you make yields more than the investment's return. This investment is made for you and your goals , and if there is a goal to earn one million dollars, you may be looking to ensure that your portfolio is well-diversified because you're unlikely to get an instant million dollars with penny stocks.

Two-Tips and Disclaimers

If you begin trading penny stocks and buying them If you start trading penny stocks, you will see newsletters and emails appearing all over the places. Beware of the "tips" that are in these publications as no one is willing to give information free of charge. The SEC requires that a business include a disclosure at the end of the article or promotion in case they are compensated or otherwise compensated by the company whose company they are marketing. Be sure to look over every promotion for the disclosure, and don't overlook the information. It's no different from buying shoes at an outlet store chain since the advertisement claims they're the most popular.

Most of the time, stocks will reach their 52-week highs, not because the business is doing well, but due to the fact that a variety of magazines picked up the ad that the company paid for. These strategies aren't worth it and could lead you to invest in stocks that is likely to crash soon after and give you a negative investment returns. Like everything else, you must conduct your own research on a company prior to when you buy and sell. Be sure to ignore any tips that are advertised and warnings about purchasing a specific shares.

Three-Speed Of Sale

One of the most costly mistakes you could make is to expect a 1,000 percent profit on the penny stock. If you hold out for this kind of performance I'm sure you'll be losing more than you earn. A healthy and safe return on a stock can be between 20 and 30 percent in just a few weeks. This kind of rate is the reason why penny stocks are so well-liked in the investment world with a steady return in a very short time. You are purchasing large quantities and selling them fast, which means you will only make a few pennies or dollars for each stock, however, you're doing it in bulk, over short time, and with very little or any effort.

The quick turnaround on penny stocks is what allows investors to get a huge weekly investment return because the time to make money is very small. But beware of the devil who is telling you to remain a little longer, because even the moment you discover that your stock is still rising it is a good thing you have saved yourself over the long term since the majority of stocks will be in returns when they reach the thirty percent threshold. Penny stocks carry extremely risky, do not increase the risk by putting yourself when you trade.

Four-Company Management

The companies that offer the shares typically have a variety of yet all fantastic opinions about their company and its future. Like the promotions, that you cannot believe everything the management team members say. Would you buy a vehicle from the owner of the company that manufactures cars because he claims it's the most reliable vehicle available? Most likely not. These companies will claim and do everything they can to convince the public to buy their shares, and some of them aren't actually legitimate companies. Many people make the appearance of a "company," sell stock and then reap the earnings of a business that is only a paper.

One of the most crucial aspects to be aware of is that, no matter what kind of stock you are trading, there will always be those who are trying to take off you. When you trade small-cap stocks, risks are greater because the rules are more limited in comparison to the standards set by the SEC. Don't trust anything until you've received the facts from a reliable source. If it appears to be too seem too good to be true it most likely is. Make sure you do your homework, know the business, and in case you're not sure, pass the stock on or talk to an expert who can guide you in the direction to follow.

Five-Short Sales

Short sales are a type of a completely different perspective on stocks. When you buy a stock you hope it will appreciate to allow you to sell the stock and earn an income. As an example, if you buy the one-quarter share X Company stock at $100 and then the following week, the shares are valued at $150. You can technically sell the stock and earn 50 percent profit on your the investment. Short selling occurs the process where an investor takes out a loan on the stock, then sells it and then waits for the price of the stock decreases to allow them to buy it back and earn the money.

For instance, Joe takes out a loan of ten shares for $50, and then sells the shares. The 500 dollars are put into his account and he then waits. If the price of the shares rises to $75 in a matter of the next week, he'll need to purchase shares again, however it will cost him money. If the shares fall to $25, he must purchase the shares, however the shares will be worth 50 percent profit. There are numerous regulations regarding the process and it is required to go through the broker.

Because of the volatility that penny stocks exhibit, it's not a wise idea to sell them short. Although some may seem appealing, you don't know if they've been increased in value due to a advertising. Both of these factors make it risky to short sell penny stocks and the results seldom exceed the risks.

Six-Volume

Based on the brokerage firm according to the brokerage firm, Penny stocks are those that cost that are priced between less than and five dollars per share. Due to their low price you should purchase the stocks in bulk to increase your return on your investment. It would be useless if you only traded just one share at a, making.30 a trade. The goal is to increase your profits and you must do this within a specific timeframe you establish when you plan your financial goals and objectives. But, you must be realistic as if you invest more than ten thousand dollars in one stock, and it falls you've made a loss of a substantial amount. Find a balance between not enough and too much share of penny stocks.

In terms of volume, it is also important to pay attention to the stocks you are purchasing. You should stick to firms that sell at least 100,000 shares each day.If you pick stocks that have less volume of trading and you could end up in a situation where it is difficult selling off the stock in the future. If a stock of a company has less than 100,000 transactions a day and doesn't have a value of more than fifty cents, you'll want to put it aside and shift to another company.

Seven-Stops

Stops were mentioned in the previous chapter, however there are two different ways to look at stop loss. The majority of people think that it's smart to use your broker's stop loss tool to protect yourself from falling to the negative when a stock isn't performing well. If you're not someone who is constantly monitoring the market, you'll be able to make use of the stop loss for each buy you've made. But there's another approach to take care of this, but it is more risky and requires self-control and self-interest.

The purpose of mental stops is you set your stops according to what you believe is the best for the share. You'll look over the shares and determine what you would like to gain out of it and take note of the point at which the cut-off is. This method requires some practice and knowledge on the market and, although it is risky, it can yield greater returns. In general, you're expanding the limits of your portfolio without a fallback plan, however, you have the ability to begin and stop at the point you think is the best.

Eight-The-Best

There is no doubt that you will always strive to acquire the most desirable option available at the moment in time. One option is to keep track of an investment and purchase the most expensive one when it reaches its fifty-two-week point, especially in the case of general growth.

This process can take several weeks, and you'll need to keep an eye on a stock for several weeks before buying it. The same dedication to this is as the effort to investigate a company prior to purchasing its shares. You must be certain of your investments, and treat every single one like it's the precious gem that can lead you to your goal.

It is sometimes difficult for a company to rise and leap, but then begin to drop when you're looking to buy however this is a something that happens. You cannot always know what an investment will be doing and, in actuality you're not able to know the way it will behave. Sometimes, a stock could be doing well and then you awake and discover that the CEO has died without an heir throwing, and then down the prices of stocks go. The patience and research, however will pay back in the end.

Nine-Large Portions

This crucial practice is vital and often overlooked. When you buy penny stocks, you're buying them in bulk but when you decide to sell the stock, you should not perform the same. In the first place, you must limit your stock's size regardless of its potential so that you're in a position to sell your stocks quickly when it begins to fall. If you are planning to sell your stock regardless of the status, it is important to spread the amount you're selling. The best general rule of thumb is to not offer more than 10 or 15% of the stock's daily volume. For instance, if you purchased the equivalent of ten thousand shares of stock, and it's time to sell them, you wouldn't want to offer all of the shares at once. If the volume per day is five thousand shares, then you should only sell 500-750 shares every day until it's gone. If you have an emergency, you may sell all the stock in one go, however it's better for you to do it in smaller batches rather than making large shares sales all at once. Some investors may view the sale as an indication that the stock isn't doing well or could do badly in the coming days, making it difficult to sell.

Ten-Keep It Professional

Be aware that there is the reason why penny stocks have earned themselves a negative reputation, regardless of the level of success you have with them. Each company will boast that they've revolutionized business, that their product are going to explode, and that there aren't any other businesses comparable to them. No matter what you research, be cautious and shrewd in your purchases of stocks. Don't be enticed by the company or stock, no matter if they're a good fit for everything they do. this isn't a wise decision.

It is also likely that when you speak to relatives and friends about the penny stock market everyone will have an opinion or some suggestions. Although they might be trying to help, you must make your own choices based on solid research and adhering to the guidelines you've established for yourself. It is vital to diversify your portfolio, not just for your general portfolio but for your penny stock portfolio, too. Be aware and do what's best for your needs and your goals, and avoid listening to the opinions of others and their opinions.

It is completely possible to earn excellent rate of return, but you must be educated about the game and keep an eye at scammers that tend to exploit the penny stock trading. Certain investors don't have the capital to buy shares of Google and so penny stocks work well for those who are. If a stock selection works out, then the investor can make huge gains. If you purchase 1,000 shares of stock priced at thirty cents and the stock rises to $1 and you make 4000 dollars. But, to be prudent you'd sell that stock when it was fifty to seventy-five cents . Then keep the return on your the investment. Sure, you'd like to get the most value for your money however, you must make it happen in a responsible method and not place bets on companies which may or might not exist at the time you get up early in the day. A stock that is waiting to double on the basis of penny stocks space is risky and seldom happens, therefore, take advantage of the profits and keep moving ahead.

This chapter will provide you with the basics and the nuances of the best practices you should be following for trading in your stock. These are only guidelines and, as time passes you'll be able include more to your list of rules and guidelines that can benefit you with penny stocks. The main theme of investing in penny stocks is to use your mind and conducting research about all the information you can find. It is also important to be aware of firms and individuals trying to rob you of your money, which could end up putting you back on your objectives. After you've gained the ability to buy and sell your penny stocks, you'll have to learn how to keep track of them in the system to take the correct decision about which stocks to sell them. It isn't always easy, however because of the high demand for stocks, many firms have devised efficient systems for tracking different stocks , all within the click of your fingers.

Chapter 9: Strategies and Strategies for Smarter Investing

Don't Short Sell Penny Stocks

You are probably familiar with the trading of options on stock exchanges that are traditional. Options of this kind are offered on penny stocks, too however they are not as popular and don't have any sense when viewed in terms of the total price per share for the stock. The price of entry is low enough that they aren't even needed but I've observed an increase in the emphasis on the idea of short selling penny stock. It is my opinion that you should Do not sell penny stock short. The practice may appear similar to buying put options on a stock, however it is in fact more risky. There are requirements for capital that must be satisfied, and you'll have to conduct a directly exchange with the company which arranged for the short. Do not do it; the cost is high, time-consuming and difficult to establish and difficult to forecast the outcome and could be financially damaging. Concentrate on earning money by trading and buying shares. Don't be concerned about alternatives for penny stocks, and especially do not short sell penny stocks.

You can make money even In the Event of Disaster

In the first chapter I discussed one of the drawbacks of penny stocks, which is the "pump and dump" strategy which is often cited by public figures and celebrities. people. One of the most recent examples of this that I could imagine is the rapper 50 Cent. He began backing the small business that was registered as penny stock. There was a notion that, with his backing that the company could grow and become a leader in the import of goods from other countries. This was actually an attempt to make a mark in the long history of schemes to dump and pump. This sounds awful and is something one would normally prefer to avoid. It's true however only if you show up way too late.

When the market was being controlled and manipulated, there were more people than the 50 cents that made money by increasing the value of a business. I know several people who earned thousands during this time. They were able get into the stock early and then sell their shares before the stock plummeted. If you held on to your cash for too long, or even if you invested too late, this stock could have turned out to be catastrophic. When I inquired with my friends how they were able to exit when they needed to and they all confessed that they were fully aware that what they witnessed was not anything other than manipulation of the market. They decided to invest as they were aware that the price was set to go up substantially and they knew when to sell as they were aware of the gap between the ask and bid prices. When they noticed the spread increase slowly and they resisted selling, the stock was beginning to become harder to dispose of. They weren't savage in the amount of money they earned and if they were then they would lose their investment.

It's a Good Thing to be Volatile

If you decide to use the day trading method it is important to look for stocks with extremely high volatility. Stocks that are performing consistently regardless of whether they are performing well, are not worth the investment for an investor in penny stocks. It's extremely difficult to make a substantial return from a stock which increases, but very slowly. It is the volatility that traders can make real money and the cyclical volatility. Find stocks with enough activity to keep the spread between bid and ask to a minimum. Keep in mind you are not in the best scenarios, you're not looking to hold the stock for very long. It is a sign that you'll be capable of selling your stock at the moment it arrives. A gradual and steady rise in the value of your stock is much less than wild swings. The wild swings are exactly the kind of thing you'd like to see.

Try a week of fake Trading

Before investing with cash I would suggest you take one or two weeks of practicing with fake trading. This is a fantastic low risk method to test the waters of investing. Get an account in a notebook and begin making up your own your own trades based upon information on the OTCBB and the NYSE. Brokerage fees are an element and for this week, just apply an 8 percent tax on any trade you execute. Take this as the amount you'd have to pay to the broker. If you're able to earn profits through fraudulent trading, then it's time to tackle the real deal. This is your chance to discover the type of trading that is most suitable for you. A week is enough time to consider whether day trading is the right choice best for your needs, or when you are enjoying it. It may take more time to figure out if value trading will more likely to bring you profits. In general, I do not hold my value trades for more than a week, but these trades may last beyond one week in the event that the market hasn't changed its mind by adjusting the value of the stock in a way that is consistent with value trading (remember it is a fact that investors who invest in value are investing in a business based on the value of the assets being higher over the cap of the company. It will only take the case that it will be a matter of time before the price of the stock reflects the actual value for the investment).

Choose the Best Broker

In the case of trading penny stocks, you'll have many options on the best online broker to pick from. Some are specialized in the OTCBB however, the majority be able to work with several exchanges. Keep in mind that I highly recommend sticking to the OTCBB as well as the NYSE. It is important to choose your broker according to the most favorable rates. For those who are new to investing I'd suggest Scott Trade, however there are other options there based on the amount that you intend to invest. The broker will charge an upfront cost that they will keep as a source of investment income. It's similar to having a bank account that is second in that is, in most cases, the more money you put in, the less your rates for trade will rise. The most important thing to do when searching for the right broker in addition to the transaction price is to determine your style of trading and working with the appropriate tools.

Brokers have a broad array of tools, which vary in the services you pick. A majority of brokers provide tools for financial analysis, however should you prefer to concentrate on trading on a daily basis, you must look for the broker with the top tools that are suitable for your needs. The tools offered typically have the exact capabilities, but the difference is in the interfaces and how you are able to compare data from a variety of sources. If you're going to solely focus on trends, then you'll need a different set tools you are comfortable with in comparison to the standard tools of the majority of traders. Determine your preferred style of trading and then choose the broker that's the best for you.

Keep a Trade Log

If there's a single point of advice from this book that can lead to higher profits over all other suggestions, it's keeping an account of your trading. The log of your trading is the most essential instrument that will ensure you long-term success in investing in penny stocks. The primary requirement for this tool is filling in sufficient details that you're able to put together all of your trades from the past. Your logbook may be in the form of a physical document or be an Word document However, it should be precise, with numbers as well as thoughts, dates and explanations for your actions. You must record every trade you execute during a specific week. It is essential to record the spread of each trade you made and what the main reasons were to justify your purchase of the particular stock, as well as the dates and reasons for what you traded and the overall gain or loss for each particular trade.

A trade log lets you identify the patterns of your trade which would otherwise be invisible to you. As a value-trader, what I've found reviewing the trade journal is some details about financials from businesses that I will never be sure of. For instance, this March, I made an investment in a startup that pioneered the concept of a VR headset. The company was partly in response to a live demo of the headset with the primary feature being that everything was wireless. I looked at the total amount of investment capital they put up and it seemed like an excellent investment. The issue was that I didn't take a take a look at the financial obligations of every single one of the employees in the company. The chief technician was in the process of filing two lawsuits, one arising from a divorce and one arising from wrongful termination from his previous employer. It's possible that you'll think it's not my issue is, and it shouldn't affect the product they are creating and, in this case, the patent that covers the wireless headset they're producing, but it's not accurate. If you are a small business you must learn about the personal liabilities of employees since they restrict the ability for employees to be productive, present and increase the chance that they will use resources from the company to settle their own legal issues. In this instance the engineer was bound to quit the company and pursue an immediate job with a higher salary to settle the legal obligations. It is my belief that his goal was to make use of the funds from his wrongful termination case to pay the legal costs associated with his divorce. It didn't go as planned and the star of the project as well as the significant work on the patent and project ended up in a dead end. This is an instance which stands out however there will be many cases of this type of tiny error that will occur during your career in trading. It is important to keep as accurate records as you can to ensure you're aware of each mistake you make and ensure that you're not at risk of repeating these mistakes again. I have learned from my own experience that I'll have to review the current obligation of law, or even request information about them for every key employee of a business. The whole concept behind the buy-and-hold strategy was based on the value of stocks rising due to a patent. It didn't happen due to the fact that I didn't conduct enough investigation into the primary technician.

Know Your Time Investment

The amount of time you are able to devote to a given week with penny stocks will determine the principal trading strategy you employ. It is essential to be real about how much time you have to devote to study, and be seated without distractions during a whole trading day. I have found that the majority of people, even those who work full-time are able to find the time to invest in the value of trading. If you're able to make time to trade during the day this is a great way to make money in the first week. Otherwise, value trading can earn you profits in the initial month. It's just a matter of identify a profitable trade, and you can be reasonably sure that you'll make profits.

Alongside the overall time commitment, you should be aware that trading is a laborious and tedious work. If you are working on value trading, then you'll have to be genuinely interested in about the industries which these firms operate and you'll need to pay attention to the information you study. The only way to achieve this is to do your research on the businesses you've chosen for value trading. Similar to day trading. In that you'll need to be aware of yourself and believe that you will be able to keep track and track your positions for a periods of between eight or 10 hours. While you're in front of your computer, it's mental exhaustion and once you begin there's an added anxiety about not knowing the capabilities of your mind.

Chapter 10: Determining the Penny Stock Scams

It's hard not to think about a penny stock that is touted as the next thing to watch. Even though it could be seen as a scam many new investors do fall for this trap. The market is flooded with publicly traded corporations on the major stock exchange. But, many people remain attracted to less well-known penny stock businesses.

A penny stock firm listed on the Over-The-Counter Bulletin Board an electronic system that displays live quotes, volume data as well as prices for last-sale securities. It is usually promoted as being on NASDAQ. However, this isn't the case however NASDAQ supervises OTCBB. However the penny stock that is listed as a part of Pink Sheets isn't regulated by any financial or government institution. Therefore, it's an investment that is more risky than other major stock company that is listed on the stock exchange. The company is prone to incur deficits and losses that are large. In addition, it could fold. An investor may check with the Securities and Exchange Commission for details on the penny stock companies.

Strategies and tools used in Penny Stock Scams

Emails that are spam or junk are often distributed by scammers to draw attention to an individual penny stock. The majority of these emails contain false information regarding the company. It is strongly advised not to purchase the stock that is advertised solely from the emails that you have received. Additionally, bulletin boards are utilized to share "hot tips" regarding a specific stock. Scammers make use of aliases to spread false information. Any investor with an interest should exercise due diligence in the event of investing in penny stocks. Certain companies employ stock promoters who offer "unbiased and impartial" advice through mass media. Before relying on these paid promoters you should verify if they hold financial credentials.

The boiler room and cold calls strategies are also employed by fraudsters that have an organised group of sales agents who are high-pressure. They use cold calls to convince potential investors to purchase the penny stock. It is recommended to be wary of calls from unknown individuals. Additionally the penny stock firm could issue fake press announcements. Anyone who is interested in investing should be sure to conduct an investigation independently to ensure that the company doesn't deceive him.

If the customer is a victim of fraud, he may complain to his broker. If this doesn't resolve the issue, the first is able to report it to the Securities and Exchange Commission or the securities regulator in the state.

The reason people become interested in Penny Stocks

A penny stock gives the possibility of excitement and the opportunity to make money quickly. It's similar to lottery tickets that offer an improved future for the winner (if it's an award-winning ticket).

Anyone who invests in penny stocks typically isn't able to use mathematical calculations to determine the value of the penny stock company's value. The investor doesn't look at the financial statements, studies on industry and dividend projections as well as discounted cash flows. Furthermore that a penny stock is an example of hidden information. A person who has an interest in a particular company often feels special since it is something people around him don't. When he discusses his investment, people will be interested because it's something that they've never heard of.

A penny stock lacks liquidity. This is the reason why many experts do not recommend purchasing this kind of stock. However, it's extremely unstable. The price could undergo wild fluctuations that provide a variety of opportunities to make money quickly. An unexperienced investor might purchase shares of penny stocks because the price is always rising. He isn't aware that he's among the people who increase the cost. If he decides to dispose of his share it soon becomes apparent that nobody wants to buy the stock any more. A person decides to put his money into a specific penny stock because he thinks that this company will become the similar to Microsoft or Wal-Mart. He is not aware the fact that these companies, who were founded with modest beginnings, have offered shares to the general public even though they had already grown to a large extent. The companies that have chosen to go public IPOs as they seek to grow their business.

These investing errors can be avoided if an investor imagines himself to be the proprietor of the company that is a penny stock. It is essential to remove his feelings out of the investment equation to be able to make an informed and rational decision. The liquidity issue isn't a major concern when the penny stock business continues to expand.

The Factors to Consider When the purchase of a penny stock

Many traditional investors have become wealthy by investing in stocks of high-quality. However, only a handful of them have made it rich through penny investment in stocks. The potential of compounding steady gains from premium stocks is the sole reason for the huge wealth of traditional investors. Their preferred companies continue to increase their revenues and profit. These companies provide high returns on shareholders' money. Dividends are usually given to shareholders. Investors buy shares continuously to boost their earnings.

However the investor of the penny stock industry is unable to raise his share due to liquidity issues. If he keeps buying shares, he'll result in the price of the share to rise. The penny stock isn't efficient and therefore, the investor is required to pay more prices for each purchase. The costs are a detriment to any earnings that an investor can make from the investment. In reality, an investor could even lose money due to these costs of friction.

Chapter 11: The General Trends in Stock Trading

General trends to study:

After you've calculated the internal variables Let's look at what external elements influence the market's direction:

Social Trends

Political Trends

- Consumer trends

- Industrial situation

- Economic conditions

The policies of the government

Global political situation

Social Trends:

The trading of penny stocks is heavily affected by the current social inclinations of the product that the company sells. Small startups could grow dramatically if their product have a huge following or completely fail when the product was simply an unpopular trend. For those companies offering services, the current trend is the regular acceptance of this segment in the world. Ford Motor Company, which was once trading at less than one dollar, has grown to a $160 billion empire.

Political Trends:

A period of political tension within a country can affect stocks as well. Political leaders determine which direction the economy, and consequently business will be through the implementation of policies. These decisions could alter the direction of markets, and they don't require large-scale modifications like presidential elections. They could be as minor as a local election for small-sized businesses which deal on penny shares. An experienced trader will keep conscious of the impact of political instability on the direction of the stock market.

Industrial Situation:

The marijuana industry has hit the jackpot when marijuana was made legal in Canada. Similar to the situation, the stocks of the coal mining sector are constantly declining due to the ongoing environmental bills through the assembly chambers all over the globe. Be aware of the general situation of the sector your targeted business is in.

Economic conditions:

Although not as impacting penny stocks, the economic environment of the base of startup of the target company could impact the earnings to price percentage of your share. A little background information can be helpful.A company that is located in countries in the third world like Pakistan as well as India is more vulnerable to a deteriorating economic situation as compared to an economically stable nation.

Competition:

The term "competition" doesn't mean only physical businesses that offer similar services or products to your company. The term can also refer to market share of the business in the field as well as market share of rival companies, and any new competition you might expect to face in the business. This is called the barrier to entry. The more difficult it is to enter an industry, the less are the odds of gaining the emergence of new competition. It's more difficult for your business to establish itself in the marketplace. For instance, the automotive industry has already picked its top producers. It's extremely difficult for a brand new business to establish its name in this industry that is brimming with stars such as Ford, Toyota, Audi, GM and many more. It is, however, relatively simple for a business to find its position in a market that is more unstable or changing. For instance, financial technologycompanies that are founded on the concept of blockchain, which was first proposed in 2009 have witnessed an exponential rise in public interest and, consequently, their price of shares. Market research is essential to understand the barriers to entry into the market. This can increase the likelihood of taking on new challenges. Always choose a high barrier to entry for businesses which have established themselves on the marketplace, for instance in industries that are complex, where all production is protected under patents and controlled by the government. If a business is beginning to grow buds, a low-end bar to entry would be suggested as it's much easier to create an entry point when the monopoly doesn't work against your. This is the case for websites, daily items like soap and toothpaste to pizza restaurants and eateries.

Examine the competitive advantage: A competitive edge occurs the case when a business is superior to its rivals due to advantages in PESTLE elements such as Economic, Political and Socio-Cultural. Technological, environmental, and legal or because they possess VRIO (Valuable rare, inimitable and organized) resource, special skills in what they do , or new capabilities that are difficult to locate or valuable. A company that has the patent of a specific method is in an extremely advantageous position in comparison to companies competing for similar products. A business located in Pakistan or India is able to reap huge benefits due to the low cost and vast labor pool.

Another aspect of competition is which is usually overlooked. Businesses purchase shares of other companies in order to safeguard their own gains and loss to their competitors. They also use this strategy to cause a ripple effect in the shares of their competitors in the exact time that they want to. Looking for shareholders of the company you're interested in is a great method to determine if competitors are attempting to acquire your target business by gradually buying their ways to the investors table.

Chapter 12: Spotting Hot Trends

In Penny Stocks

Within the realm of trading stocks When you notice an ebullient trend, take it on! It is sensible to follow this recommendation. Of course, you need to be aware of the time to pull back also, but typically, when a stock does well, it will remain that way for a certain duration. We hope that it lasts long enough to allow you to profit from your investment.

The trends are positive, however, how do you identify trends and possibly forecast their future? These are the perennial questions that are posed to investors. If they could solve this, they'd be billionaires. There are still ways to identify trending penny stocks in a hurry. Here are a few of them: most effective:

1)Learn to recognize price patterns. If you notice that the trend of the last couple of weeks has been upwards, then shares are likely of sustaining that growth. In contrast, if you see it going down, expect that same, but in the case of a decrease. A trend is simply the tendency to move in either way or the other for a specific period of time. If you are able to identify an emerging trend, you should take advantage of it.

2)Once you have identified trends in the price of penny stocks, place yourself in a place to profit from it. The most common rule is to buy the penny stock when it is on their upward trend. Because you are aware that how penny stocks are going upwards, take advantage of it! Take the plunge and be sure to profit from the good things.

3)Know when to get rid of. The best strategy for penny stocks and analyzing the current trends is to determine when you should end your investment. Every investor is aware that staying over your comfort zone with stocks that are falling can result in loss. This is the thing that every investor tries to avoid. It is a rule that all good things have to come to an end. That means that no matter how much your penny stock is outperforming all the other stock options in the past, eventually it will not.

4)Check forums. Chatrooms and forums are a excellent way to keep current with the is trending and what to look for. Of course when I refer to forums, I don't mean to reading what they're talking about, I'm talking about actually getting involved chat with others who have more knowledge than you do. Also, when when you're a professional you may also be the one people turn to for assistance. Participating in a community can aid you in growing more quickly than simply being all around the world.

The trend can be correlated to two aspects such as trading volume and price of shares. Let's say for instance, the share price of a penny stock is experiencing more volume of trading over the past five weeks. This could be an indication of a growing volume, and could mean more movement from investors. The prices may soon be increasing gradually as a consequence.

In order to identify trends take a look at the charts for trading. If you can see an upward trend that means it is in an upward trend. If you notice a downward trend however, the reverse is also true. The smallest, or even the largest changes can be dismissed. It is important to have a bigger perspective when looking for the best way to spot trending penny stock. Make sure to expand your view to be able to see trends. Certain trends do not show up in penny slots when you look at a 3-week span however, if you extend your view to a three-month time frame, you could be able to capture a significant trend to profit from.

Chapter 13: Penny Stocks In The US

When an investor buys an asset, the buyer anticipates a return and maybe eventually sell the asset for an attractive cost, a value that is higher than the buyer originally bought it. There are many different types which can be classified as assets. They are classified under the term "asset categories." The classes of assets have traits that are comparable to other investments. The primary asset classes you need to become familiar with are equities, commodities cash equivalents, real estate. Be aware that each principal asset class includes an associated sub-category which is distinct from the other. In this section, we're going to talk about US penny stock. We'll also look at how the US penny stocks to new market stocks. We'll go over the features of each are, as well as how different they are from each other and how appropriate they are. Read on to find more.

"Emerging market" are those that come up in emerging markets that are growing quickly and are characterized by favorable demographics. They are known for their growing economic output as well as capitalization on the stock market. IMF declares that countries like this make up an important portion of world's total output, approximately 40 percent in dollars, to be precise. The countries classified as "emerging" include Latin America, Asia, Africa, Middle East, and Eastern Europe. Additionally, there are emerging markets that are called "BRIC," meaning they are the countries comprising Brazil, Russia, India and China. The BRIC are thought of as impressive emerging markets.

In the past these economies have attracted large quantities of institutional and retail investors. The emerging markets are typically different from US stock markets. Investors stand a greater chances of earning high returns if they concentrate their attention on emerging markets, while also pursuing new opportunities. The benefit of these areas is that they have a lot of young workers, very high level of domestic consumption, less government debts, and an excellent potential for growth of industrial output. Remember that retail penetration of these economies is very low and they are extremely volatile with very little trading volume, in comparison with other countries. If you choose to invest in emerging markets, be sure to be aware and pay close attention to the current economic and political circumstances that are taking place in each nation. If you choose to invest, you're strongly encouraged to purchase emerging market stocks directly from the brokerage company. You can, however, make investments on your own by investing in big trading US firms, such as those that issue the American Depository Receipts (ADR).

US Penny Stocks in the US are a bit different from emerging stocks. They are extremely inexpensive, yet they are also extremely risky. The number of investors who are keen on them is large, and competition could be quite competitive. The purchase of penny stocks isn't an issue, however selling them is a different matter. It's very difficult to trade penny stocks because of their lack of quantity and liquidity, as well as their huge spreads of big-ask. Let's discuss this issue for a bit to find out the ways in which US penny stocks compare to emerging stocks.

From an investment perspective: US penny stocks trade for a brief period of time, whereas emerging markets trade over a long length of time.

The speculative aspect of penny stocks the speculation about investment and market conditions is extremely high. Contrarily, with emerging stocks, which have a lower percentage of speculation.

The Regulatory Authority: US penny stocks report for the Securities and Exchange Commission located in the United States while the reports emerging stocks report to the Securities and Exchange

Commission based on the country in which they are investing in.

Predictability: Although penny stocks are extremely easy to predict, the emerging stocks are not as easy to predict.

Valuation: The penny stocks do not offer "real" value as the shares typically cost about $.10. Emerging stocks are sure to have worth since huge amounts of cash are able to be invested with confidence at any given time.

Spread: As mentioned earlier, the spread of the big-ask is huge for penny stocks, which makes trading difficult for them. Emerging stocks do not have a wide spread, which makes trading much more simple.

Platform to trade: US stocks trade on the OTC market, while new stocks are traded on exchange stocks of the nation they are trading on. There are a variety of trading platforms.

Amount of data that is available to investors is very little publicly available information about US penny stocks which can make them extremely uncertain. They don't have to submit periodic or annual reporting that means they are less transparent and have less rules. When you conduct your research prior to investing you won't be able find written analyst reports for this type of US penny stock. Emerging stocks on the other hand, are able to provide information that is continuously and continuously regularly updated. Emerging stocks stay up to date with the standards of reporting and have very transparent data and are able to publish numerous analyst reports.

Fundamental Analysis: It's an extremely difficult task using fundamental research to analyze penny stock since they are not able to provide information or report. However, the opposite is true in the case of emerging stocks, where there's plenty of information about the financial history of a company and its economic situation.

Caps The Penny stocks are small-sized caps, and emerging stocks are available in all forms small, medium and large.

Can they be worth it? US penny stocks come the risk of a high risk/reward ratio, but this risk may be worthwhile at times. The risk associated with investing in emerging stocks is moderate that is, it's estimated and could also bring large or moderate amount of money to investors.

What do they mean to investors The emerging stocks are found and traded across a variety of countries, making them more geographically diverse. They can offer many opportunities for growth to the top companies for future development. US penny stocks, however, can be great for those who are an investor who is just beginning their journey or a trader. US penny stock investments can be carried out at the convenience of your own home or with an expert brokerage company but they don't have the potential to be economically or financial and are therefore risky and inadvisable for new investors.

Chapter 14: Technical Analysis

In the case of analytical techniques, the primary thing to remember is that it's effective due to its belief that price fluctuations over time is an accurate indicator of price changes in the near future. Contrary to fundamental analysis it is not necessary to wait for specific data to be revealed because there's already more data on technical analysis available than you can ever hope to get through yourself. This plethora of information can be analyzed using indicators such as charts, trends, and charts to ensure that you don't enter into a transaction without a evidence that it will result in a profit.

Although some of the information discussed below may seem a bit obscure, when you get right to it, what you're looking for is significant future trends. Spend some time and you'll soon be able to read technical charts with the highest quality.

The fundamentals are: First of all Technical analysis lives and dies according to the things it can determine about the trade in question by its resemblance to a pattern from the past that isn't obvious to a vast number of people. If you want to achieve success with the analysis of technical aspects, you'll want to try to make sure that three things are present to ensure the most effective outcomes. First The market is bound to devalue all things at certain points. Furthermore, trends and price are interconnected, so they are always a sign to the next. The final point is that history will repeat itself if you have an extended timeframe.

It is due to these three principles that those who advocate of technical analysis come to the conclusion that the price that an individual stock is trading for is the sole metric to be taken into consideration since it is a synthesis of all that is happening around the globe that impacts the specific stock. This means that once you have a good idea of what the current price is of the stock you're looking to buy, then you will are able to access all information regarding the economic situation overall. This is important because the analysis of technical aspects also suggests that all prices change in accordance with a range of various trends that have been identified. This means that all you have to do is locate the correct one and then you are able to accurately determine the stock that you are interested in is likely to do in the near future.

While it may seem somewhat preposterous but it's really an effect of the reality that there are many stocks to pick from, and it's more likely for an existing pattern to repeat than for a completely new pattern to be developed, particularly in the case of historical data on stocks accessible. If this occurrence is paired together with the notion that human beings are naturally drawn to patterns, you get an extremely useful measurement that not only describes the what a trend is to be for the company in which you've spotted it, but can be able to tell you the likely actions your competitors are likely to do to address it. If this seems unlikely, consider that a number of the first technical analysis patterns , which were discovered over 100 years ago are using in the present.

Find the trend: Knowing what a trend can mean to a penny stock trading is going to be an essential technique to master if expect to be successful over the long haul. Although you should be searching for the most powerful trends that you can however, you must be aware that they can range from weak to powerful, with certain trends being so faint as to be totally irrelevant, while others are so powerful that they're impossible for anyone to ignore. It is essential to keep this in mind, and do your research to search for patterns that are already in existence while taking care not to give any significance to patterns that don't exist in reality.

The best way to determine the pattern you're seeing is actually there is to find an array of lows and highs that are placed in a big enough number of groups to demonstrate that a pattern is present beyond any shadow of a doubt. The removal of the middle part of a particular pattern is likely to allow you to identify its general utility. However, this doesn't mean that a pattern is going to have every high or low but instead, you'll know that you're on the right path if you observe a variety of highs that are higher than prior highs, referred to as an uptrend, or lows that follow previous lows which is known as a reverse. If you spot patterns that have at least an equal amount of highs and lows the pattern you've found is called horizontal trends.

If you come across an underlying trend that seems to be lasting longer with each cycle, the most likely thing is that the following cycle will be also longer, but at the same time getting ready for the inevitable reverse. If you discover an apparent trend to be very small, the first thing you're likely to check is that it's not part of any longer trend you're not being able to see. The most effective way to accomplish this is to examine the longer period of charts and then see what is a result of it. This can result in the process taking much longer than it would normally be, it is essential to make sure that you aren't making decisions based on inaccurate data. Similar can be said regarding switching to charts with smaller time frames since looking at trends under an microscope can help to understand previously unintelligible data.

Then, once you've discovered the trend you're after The next step will be to create a trendline that will serve as a means of determining the trends you've discovered. To create a trendline, all you have to do is draw an uniform line across the data points you're interested in, focusing on the high points of negative trends and the low points of positive trends. What you have made is known as a resistance line , and it's physical symbol of the market's capacity to repress the penny stock of interest whenever it is too high or low. Although it is not always helpful in forecasting what the stock you are considering will do in the future but it can help you understand the general limits to what the stock is likely to change.

After you have completed drawing the main line, then the second step you'll need to to draw a line each side of the trend line to indicate the ancillary levels of resistance as well as support. The channel can then be moving positively, negatively, or horizontally. If you extend the channel to a sufficient time, you'll be able to identify where the price will be able to diverge from its norm. This signifies the time frame in which you'll likely have to move if you are looking to earn the highest profits you can.

Chapter 15: Keys To Profit in

Penny Stocks

This is the moment to reached the portion of this book , where you'll learn everything you need to learn about starting your penny stock trading business. You may believe that trading penny stocks is complicated with all the regulations, things to keep an eye on complex terms used in stock exchanges and more is not the case, however it's straightforward. Follow the steps below for the four most fundamental steps to begin your venture with penny stocks.

Research

As you would when with something you're not sure of, the very first thing you must conduct is research. This book is a good example of the word "research" can describe two different types of research. Before you go to war, you need to get your weapon prepared and, with penny stocks there's nothing more valuable than knowing information as your weapon.

The first step is to conduct general research. This is the process of collecting general information on penny stocks, including what is it, how to do it, and the most important thing is the risk associated with it. This is a subject that's already covered within this guide. By this, you have the necessary knowledge to conduct the general penny stock research.

The other research is specific research on stocks. This type of research should be carried out when you're already seeking out investment opportunities in penny stock. Doing research on the stocks you plan to invest in must be conducted when working with all sorts of stocks but it is more crucial when it comes to penny stock. This happens because as you see from the previous chapters, information regarding penny stocks is a bit lacking and hard to come across in comparison to other types of stocks.

When you are researching penny stocks there are two elements that you must look for. First search for any public information on the stock. The other thing to seek out is information about the past performance of the stock. To find this information it is important to look back and keep track of the types of events that happened as well as the reaction to the share price. A good example are instances where the price of the shares remained at what it was, even though there could be an increase. This kind of situation could suggest that investors have reviewed the information on the stock and have decided to stay away of investing in the stock.

Select a broker to set up an online Brokerage Account

Once you've done your research to the required level then the next step to complete to start investing in penny stocks is to open an account with a brokerage firm like you would an account at a bank. The brokerage account will be the place that you'll be able buy stocks as well as other investments. This is also where your money is held alongside your investments. When you buy shares the money is taken from your account and redeemed for corporate shares. If you sell your shares, they will be converted into cash.

There are a variety of brokerage accounts available. There are accounts you can manage on your own, however this isn't recommended for those who are new to the business. If you are a beginner penny stock investor like yourself, it's ideal to pick an agent. They will be those who direct buy or sell your shares according to what they are instructed. However, of course you must allocate them their payments, which are referred to as commissions or commission fees'. These fees can range from just five dollars and can go as high as hundreds.

There are two kinds of stock brokers you can pick from: Full-service stock brokers, also known by their traditional names and discounted stock brokers.

Full service brokers provide greater variety of services, such as providing advice and recommendations regarding which shares to buy and which investment is better for your business. Because of these options traditional brokers typically charge a higher commission when compared with discount brokers. The use of these types of stock brokers is best for investors who are planning to only make a couple of trades, and who are not able to pay a large amount of cash. If you are concerned about money for you, utilizing an all-inclusive stock broker isn't recommended. Commission charges for brokers like theirs can run you hundred dollars to purchase stocks, and another hundred dollars for selling. This doesn't even include any additional service charges.

An excellent option for novice investors is to work with low-cost stock brokers. Although they provide a limited range of services however, they allow you more flexibility in your the decisions. If you want to be more autonomous in your decisions, you ought to consider hiring discounted stock brokers, since their services are limited to providing very limited advice on investing. Therefore, their commissions are lower and you as an investor could save money.

An alternative that is better for you is discount online brokers that are partnered by an account for online brokerage. Utilizing the power of internet today is a great advantage. Since you'll be the main person responsible for managing your account, using web-based tools is best method of doing this. Online brokerage platforms can aid you in keeping the watch on your account and send orders to your broker. You can view the market indexes and open buy orders and be informed of quotes for stock prices, and have access to analysis and research conducted by your broker at anytime you wish to aid you in making your choices. This arrangement will allow you to reduce a significant amount from commissions while at the same time facilitate your transactions.

Once you've decided on an agent the process of setting the brokerage account will be much simpler. It is all you need to do is contact your broker(s) and they will supply you with the necessary forms or files to be completed. The majority of the time, they'll be the person who opens the account. However, it is not possible to create an account without making the initial cash deposit or the minimum amount of investment. This could be anything from one hundred dollars to over a thousand. Once you have this the account is functioning within three or four days and you'll be able start investing at that point.

Buy

If you've already established your brokerage account The next step is to begin purchasing stocks. The most important element of your trading in penny stocks. If you make a error of investing in the incorrect stocks, it's immediately and instantly that you're already likely to lose funds.

The process of buying stocks is simple. If you are looking to buy stocks it is best to first call your broker to place the purchase order. However, before you do this it is important to ensure the account of your broker is set with the right amount of cash, sufficient to cover for the costs of the shares as well as commissions you'll eventually be liable for.

If you contact your broker, you should have done your research and you have the following details including the ticker symbol of the company that issued the stock, the exchange where the stock is trading on the number of shares or the amount you would like to acquire as well as the price that you're prepared to purchase and lastly, the duration of your order or the time you would like it to run (it may be only the day you selected or up to the date you chose).

It is the symbol for trading that companies are identified on bulletin boards and exchanges. As an example, you can explain to your broker that are looking to buy 1000 shares from a particular company that has the ticker symbol HYPO for one dollar, or less that.You may also explain that the stock trades on the Bulletin Boards of OTC, and you wish for this purchase to remain in force until Thursday. At this point, all you must do is to wait, and it's the broker's responsibility to handle the transaction.

In the event that the cost of HYPO shares falls in value to, or lesser than your broker will then purchase shares. If you go to your brokerage account on the internet you'll find that you have already 1,000 shares. Therefore, the funds in your account, which serves as payment for the shares as well as the broker's commission will also be sent to the recipients of the shares for the shares, which in this case is $1000 to HYPO and approximately $5 towards your broker.

However, how do you know whether a penny stock is a worthwhile choice for investment? The following information can help to answer the question. Four things you must look at in penny stocks are:

The price range has to be 50 cents to two dollars. Prices that are more than two dollars in the Over the over the counter Bulletin Board is a bit more difficult to locate.

The average daily volume should be at least 100,000 shares. The details of this will be discussed in the following chapter.

The stock are expected to be rising on the market.

Avoid investing in companies that have negative earnings growth rates. This information is available in reports made available to the public by the SEC or in the listings.

Sell

Similar to purchasing penny stocks selling penny stocks quite simple, but it's not as simple. As we discussed in the third chapter of the book, which discussed the advantages and dangers of penny trading finding an investor for penny stocks is difficult. But having a broker handle the actual trading can make the process a lot more simple.

Like buying, all you have to do selling your penny stocks is conduct some research, get in touch with your broker and then execute the sell order. The information you gave your broker to complete your purchase order is similar to what you'll have to provide to them when you submit the sell request. This includes: the ticker symbol, the market, the number of shares you'd like to sell, the price of the shares, and lastly the duration of your order.

For instance an example, you can inform your broker of the fact that you would like to transfer from your account 1,000 shares to a specific company, using an HYPO ticker symbol. Then, you can inform them that the shares are listed on the OTCBB and that you would like to sell the stocks for the price of two dollars or more with the order remaining open until the next Wednesday.

In other words, if the price of HYPO is reached at the level of at least two dollars the stock is traded. The amount exchanged for this stock is deposited into your account. This money could later be used to fund another purchase, but the money already taken out of the broker's commission. Thus, you now have $1,995 within your accounts.

If you're interested in knowing whether you made money from your transactions , or not, then you should visit websites for investment and stocks to determine your earnings or do the calculations yourself. To calculate this, take a look at the money you spent to purchase the order and the amount you paid out for the sale order. In this case, for instance, if your purchase cost you 1 005 ($1,000 to purchase the stock, and $5 for commission fees) And you received $1,995 from your sell-order ($2,000 in stocks subtracted by $5 to cover the commission fee) and after subtracting the commission fee, you will make the profit of $990!

Chapter 16: What to Locate Legit Penny Stocks

Every aspect of penny stock comes with its advantages and cons.You must determine which company is the best one that you should invest money into. A young, trendy and new firm is the perfect one for you to put your money into. If one buys inventory from the newly formed business for pennies, and then holds them in the bad times until the company is established, they might be capable of selling them for top prices and earn an excellent amount of profit out of those penny stocks. Here's how to succeed with new companies.

Do your research thoroughly and only invest in businesses that you are confident in and have something of value

Buy with a sum of capital (good capital) that is safe even with the risk. If you lose, it, it won't hurt you financially. Make investments that will help you to buy shares with low costs.

Make sure you hold your stock for a long time because penny stocks will pay dividends only over the long haul If you can keep them throughout the initial difficult years of your business. Prices will rise as businesses expand, grow and exceeds targets.

Analysis of the company

The correct and complete information regarding the company can help in making the right choices. Here are a few of the most crucial details to learn about the business you are planning to put your money into.

The type of business that the company is involved in. This can help you to determine how feasible and realistic the business's plans are.

The business plan of the company and its viability. Make sure that the company is able to achieve its goals.

The level in competition, and the degree of competitiveness the business is in comparison to its main competitors.

The structure of management in the business. Are they able to run the business effectively to generate profits, and are they able to manage the company effectively? capabilities?

The kind of cash flow and capitalization the business has, and your feelings about how these important elements are managed.

The general rule is that information about a company is vital because you don't wish to invest in a business that isn't legitimate.

Chapter 17: Strategy and Strategies To Maximize Your Profit

You must have the right mindset

The mentality for the top traders is one of need and not one of necessity. What I am referring to is that you should not enter a market in the belief that it is necessary to succeed. You can follow the guidelines for how to do this including using the rule of ten per cent as well as the possibility of diversification. This also illustrates the concept of the trends that are expected of an investor. An investor who is successful isn't completely right all the time. They always make bad trades which will cost the money. The most important thing is that over time, they are more successful in their trades than ones that fail. They want every trade to go to their advantage, however, they don't feel that they require the trade to be to their advantage. Being flexible and planning for the long term isn't easy in the beginning when you're just beginning to learn. My advice is to begin the penny-stock market with an investment amount of at least $2000 and then stick to the 10% rule. It is a good idea to keep an account of your trades and looking over your trades in the past, and you'll be on the path to becoming a successful trader over the long term, which is the most important quality of a good trader overall.

Do not pay for advanced trading Tools

I decided to eliminate an entire section of this book concerning brokerage firms and the best places to go. the most appropriate place to begin trading. I thought about the value of this information to new investors and I think that the most important lesson is to always choose a broker that offers the highest rates. I would suggest Scottrade for instance, since they are able to access OTCBB, NYSE and offer affordable rates. One thing I wouldn't pay more for brokerage charges so I can utilize their advanced analysis tools. This is the primary way that brokers use to charge higher fees to their clients. They provide tools to enhance your ability to manage trades using an analysis that is custom. I believe that this doesn't really justify the price for traders who are just beginning their journey. Every brokerage firm has tools that are suitable to identify trends in day trading. The additional fees you pay for the most advanced tools is an expense that, in reality almost all traders don't utilize. It takes an enviable amount of time to understand the complexities of simple tools for analysis, let aside the more sophisticated ones.

In short, pick the brokerage that has the lowest rates. I would suggest beginning with Scottrade in case you really don't know which one to choose. Once you've chosen one broker, you'll have to invest at least an hour or two playing around with the analysis tools that they provide. It is essential to master the basics of the tools that allow you to look at the prices that have been recorded for the stock, compare tools and much more. The more sophisticated tools will not aid in increasing your profits since you're just starting out and aren't really worth the additional costs for. The margins you earn when you're just beginning your journey are going to be so small that brokerage charges can quickly consume your profits.

Keep a trade log

I love trading penny stocks. I am a fan of the lifestyle. I like working at my own pace and I enjoy the thrill of deciding which businesses should invest my capital in. One aspect of trading that I completely dislike however, I do understand its importance and have a strong belief in the method You must keep a track of your trades. I briefly mentioned this in chapter 3, but it's worth repeating in this article: you must keep a journal of every trade you've made. The details in your trade log should include the cost per share, the investment and the loss or profit at the conclusion of the transaction, and more importantly, it should be able to justify why you decided to invest in the first in the first place. Whatever strategies you choose to use, you should provide reasons that are simple to comprehend for the reason you chose this investment regardless of whether it is the latest data, or data on the financials.

This is perhaps the most difficult part of trading, but equally the most crucial. It is important to periodically check through your log of trades and note where you've committed mistakes, as well as when you've had excellent results. The most helpful indicators I have on my log of trades an entry that reflects my personal opinion on each trade. It's a nifty measurement but it has really helped me to understand that my gut feeling has nothing to do with whether the trade was a smart one. My log of trades has taught me not to make a trade on the basis of my gutfeeling, which may be totally untrue for another trader. It is important to note that you will never be able to identify what your weaknesses and strengths are until you keep track of this information in a log of trades. You will be making so many trades within the first few months that recollecting any trade might appear like a blur. You must keep a track of trades otherwise you'll forget the reason you made an exchange, and you won't be able to identify your competitive edge.

Make a point of focusing on day Trading If You have A Small Investment Fund

However, even if buying and holding method ends to be the most profitable strategy for trading, you'll want to begin day trading, especially if you have only a modest amount of money to invest. Although this strategy requires large blocks of time and full days of work but it also has the most minimal capital requirements. The most important thing is that your profits are determined within one to two days after you trade. If you only have a modest money investment, you will require this instant feedback. Also, you must replenish your fund as quickly as possible in order to conduct additional trades. Day trading can take some time to master and the time requirements are a burden for many new traders. I suggest you focus on trading for four or five days per month at the beginning, if you have commitments elsewhere that require you to dedicate a full day to trade.

In addition It can be tempting to take part in trading on the aftermarket when you do not have the time to engage in trading during the day. I highly recommend to not engage in trading in the aftermarket in case you're just beginning to learn about penny stocks. While I won't go into all the details the main issue is one of insufficient information to discern patterns. It is essential to have a continuous update of information that results from the large amount of traders being in operation at the same time. Stick to trading during the daytime to begin.

Chapter 18: Comprehensive

Analyse For Penny Stock Trading

We've looked into what analysis isabout short-term stock sales, same-day sales that have set percentages. To analyze these, it is not necessary to do any deep research, since the thing we're looking for is to take advantage of the manner in which charts work. When we trade these stocks, we'll produce a daily 10% average return on our investment, assuming everything goes according to plan. It is essential to understand that when selling stocks, the money is sent to a cooling down and by dividing the total amount you invest it is possible to have cash flowing from the cool down, and invest every day and keep the cash flowing.

But, in the morning's analysis, you came across Moby Dick today. A gigantic white whale that you can put your money into the long or mid-term. How can you tell if that this isn't a fraud? Conducting a series of thorough research that can identify the credibility of the business you're investing in. This is not a matter of day trading, but rather more sophisticated strategies that may take advantage of initial stock prices to ride the trend for weeks, days as well as months. This type of scenario can occur at least once or twice per year when you discover a firm that can provide you with profits that exceed 500% in the short-term. The majority of times, you get the initial price in the boom period for a huge contract and then sell it after the publication of your income statement based on the profits made by this venture.

Income statements are a record of information that is that relate to the company's earnings. If we examine the statements, we are able to understand the actual value of the income. When buying stocks that are long-term in nature and you do so since income is vital. A business that has a large agreement with another firm is one that has a good reputation and indicates a growing financial and trade operations. A significant flow of cash doesn't reveal anything about the company but the flow of earnings within an industrial area will. Many companies that one million dollars worth of penny stocks, and make less than a tobacco seller, indicating the poor efficiency of the company they're investing in. The company could move huge numbers, and then spend more, therefore you need be sure to look over all the graphs carefully.

If you examine the formulas used by the balancers can also create cash flow statements. They can be used to detail the manner in which the company's funds was used, as well as the employee percentages and general expenses. They also provide information on how money flows into the business and the income earned from manufacturing and service operations in a way that is tacit. Stable businesses earn profits through registered operations because this is how they are able to raise funds. The finding of these kinds of indicators and then letting them run with a mere 10% profit may be the stuff of your goals for years since we're talking about a firm which in a short period of time can generate huge numbers and not only pennies. These charts will be able to see that stocks are steady, with healthy interest and volume, as well as new heights as the weeks go by. It also shows huge volumes of stock trading and a sign that interest is not declining.

It is essential to be aware of the game played by the market If your company doesn't show steady growth, and then a sudden rise, it could be the right time to sell. In the event that you hold some stocks you bought at the tiny fraction of the cost which could have remained steady for a short period of time following the gap following a major negotiations, we could find ourselves facing a market explosion to benefit from its stability. In this case, you must give up your position to the Great White Whale and sell its oil on the overpriced market. At the time of your previous stability, you could have made 400% of what you put into it prior to the profits boom due to stabilised trades. And by the time you pump, you may be able to earn 100 percent and even more from this stability figure. This is the time to earn $100.000 with a single move.

This is accomplished by studying the typical gaps of the industrial sector. Be aware that even if you're taking the case of a small company that has been resizing itself There will come an instance when the increase of its value won't match the growth of the company's actual. A niche's peak tends to follow certain patterns. When you are purchasing.

When the stock was sold at the time of the takeover in the company, it took place at much lower prices than that maintained throughout the period of holding and an increase ahead of the incoming information, and forecasting the release of income and any foreseeable periodic peak will be the main factors to take into when deciding time to make the big sale. Be patient for the next day when there could be a new peak with a slower growth of a breakout. This is when short sellers try to hedge positions. Peaks don't last for long therefore it's an anxious morning in the middle of a period of high volatility that you can sell your shares for a huge amount.

Chapter 19: The Myths about Penny Stocks

There is no doubt that there are a lot of misconceptions about a subject. The same is true for penny stocks. There are a lot of misconceptions about it, and it is essential to know the truth about these and decipher the truths so that you can invest in the right penny stocks. This chapter will examine the various myths we have discussed in this chapter to help you better understand the subject.

It's not simple to purchase and sell these stocks.

There is a widespread belief that it is hard to purchase and sell penny stocks. The belief is that you must be a fervent investor or a seasoned to be able to trade these stocks. This is just an assumption. There is a consensus that penny stocks can be somewhat difficult to find, however that doesn't make them an easy sell. If you are aware of how to trade the market and are comfortable with the notion of paper trading , it's going to be a breeze for you. It is only necessary to be aware of the functions of the penny stocks and be able to trade them.

Large firms were in the past penny

There is a widespread belief that large companies such as Microsoft were penny stocks in the past but have become billion dollar businesses. This isn't the case. It is not the case that every company transitions from being the penny stock to regular stock. When a company's size is large, and has a large market cap, then it will get listed on a large per-share price. The penny stocks are usually used by small businesses that don't have large market caps. But that doesn't necessarily mean they aren't able to be traded in huge quantities. There is no limit on the number of sellers and buyers that can exchange their shares in one day. If the company has gained recognition, then a lot of investors are likely to put money into it regardless whether it's micro or small firm.

These stocks can be fraudulent.

A lot of new investors will believe they are frauds. They'll base their belief on the price that is low for these stocks and the speed at which some of them go. In reality, at times the volume of these stocks are so small that suspicion is likely to surface. However, it's not true to believe that. The market for stocks encourages the sale of all kinds of stock. From those listed at $100 per share to those listed at less than $5. It is not important how big or small the business is. There may be fraud, however their presence is extremely minimal in the marketplace.

Prices won't fall much further.

Don't fall for the trap of thinking that the prices of these stocks won't fall in the near future. It is not possible to set a lower price limit for certain stocks. They could continue to dip before being removed. Don't believe that the value of a stock won't decrease any further. If you believe that even with a dip, it's still a great company to invest in , then you should consider investing in it. However, if you're not certain about the company then avoid it.

Prices will surely rise

There is no. There is no assurance that prices that have fallen will be able to rebound. It's all dependent on the supply and demand of the stocks as well as the extent to which they are traded in the market. There is no reason to keep keeping a stock in the market for too long. If the price hasn't increased, then you should dispose immediately.

Penny stocks are a safe bet

Many believe it's a good idea for investors to buy penny stock. However, there are a few risks associated in penny stocks. It is important to be aware of these risks before you make a decision to invest in these types of stocks. In all honesty there is no investment choice in the world that does not carry the risk. Therefore, it's absurd to think that penny stocks are secure investments. You must identify ones that make good investments and stay with the ones you like. It will become feasible after a time and after you've been studying your market over a couple of monthsor even years.

You must be an insider

There is a myth that says one must be an insider in the business to buy or be aware of the stock. However, this isn't the case. You could be a non-expert and still be aware of the top options to buy. If it's difficult to purchase these stocks due to the higher demand from buyers and lower volume, then you must find the most profitable time to buy the stocks. Experience will also aid you in determining and letting you know when the ideal time to buy into the market.

It is recommended to put money into undiscovered opportunities

Don't make the mistake of investing in companies that are not well-known believing that it is an investment that is safe. There is no guarantee in the stock market , and it's not an appropriate choice investing in a company that's emerging. What happens if it proves to be a negative company or slow to grow? You shouldn't be in a company that is not performing well. Therefore, the best option is to invest in a company which is performing very well, or that has solid track of performance.

I'd prefer not to have them.

There is no need to worry about it. It's a myth you need to fight. If you believe it's not an ideal idea to add penny stocks in your portfolio , you're wrong. These might be lower priced , but they can aid to diversify your investment portfolio. They are capable of bringing you more and more lucrative profits when opposed to the traditional stocks. Don't fall into the trap of thinking they are not as worthy. They're quite valuable and can assist you in increasing your profits margins.

There are many misconceptions surrounding the subject and it is essential to know the basics of these if you are looking to be successful in the penny stock market. It is possible to go over these once more if you feel you're not understanding the subject more.

Chapter 20: Trading Penny Stocks

Risky investments have become the preferred choice for many stock traders because of the potential for huge returns, if things go according to your strategy. When investing in penny stocks, you are investing in the stocks of small-sized businesses with an excellent potential for growth. There is no assurance that these companies will be successful in the marketplace, however in the event they succeed, investors stand to profit greatly from the investment. Penny stocks are extremely risky since these small businesses could fall at any time, which means you risk losing the entire amount you've invested in it.

Trading penny stocks is, therefore, very risky and needs to be considered before putting your funds into the investment. If you've already researched them thoroughly and decided on a strategy that you want to begin trading.

Develop your trading strategy

A successful stock trading experience is mostly dependent on the trading strategy that one employs and this isn't atypical for penny trading. It is essential to have a strategy to invest in penny stocks that you stick till the end to reach your goals for trading at the final. It is essential to be ready for the possibility of risk when dealing with this type of investment. A lot of penny stocks have been considered as unsuitable for investment by experienced traders, and you must know right from the start the risks you're facing. The truth is, only a tiny proportion of penny stocks will yield investors a decent return.

The kind of strategy you use to trade is determined by a range of variables:

Your investment needs

Due to the high risk they aren't recommended for long-term investors. If you have long-term saver plans it may not be wise to invest in these types of stocks. The risk of losing money is high, and if you're planning to save for the future, you might lose the entire amount of money within a matter of minutes. If you're looking for short-term requirements for investment in contrast you can do very well with penny stock investments. These types of stocks are ideal for those who like to sell and buy frequently.

Your restrictions

There are some restrictions that can be difficult to resolve and investors need to consider these when deciding how they'll invest in penny stocks. If , for instance, there are stocks of an organization that you can't invest in, it is essential to select a strategy that is not compromising on this. Certain traders or investors have been able to inherit stocks and do not want to sell them because of personal reasons. You must be aware of this in order to know which stocks to trade.

Your risk tolerance

Similar to all different types of stocks There are penny stocks which have higher risk than other kinds. Some stocks are characterized by high trading volume which makes them more secure than stocks with low trading volume. It is important to be shrewd in making your decision. To make sure that you balance the risk you're willing to accept with the type of profits you're expecting. Find out what you're willing to go so that you get the type of return you're hoping to earn from that investment. This should help you determine what kind of strategy you need to invest with.

Your return expectations

Every investor has a different kind of expectation regarding every investment they make. What kind of returns you anticipate from your investment portfolio in stocks will direct you to the type of strategy that is suitable for you. There are a lot of differences between people in what they expect from their investments that is why there are a variety of strategies that are suitable for different penny stock investors. What kind of returns you desire will also determine what your strategies for trading ought to be since you must be able to meet your goals at the end of the day.

Always be prepared to take a loss

Penny stocks are incredibly cheap in comparison to high-value securities. The principal reason this happens so is that they are always at a huge chance of losing. Many businesses fail and investors are able to lose a significant amount of their investment. Investors must remain aware to ensure that if it does happen they are not greatly affected. This is the reason it is recommended to diversify your portfolios when you invest in these stocks. Some companies succeed at the end of the day, which implies that you could earn some decent returns in the end However, you must be prepared for the worst that could occur so that you can be able to accept the result and continue to live your life with confidence.

Purchasing Penny Stocks

Once you are aware of the companies you plan to invest in and you've got your strategy for trading well-defined It is now time to start making the first investment. You'll require an investment account to make this purchase. Sign up with a trading platform to begin trading right away. You must ensure that you're registered with an online trading platform that will provide the ability to trade penny stock there are some that don't allow trading on penny stocks.

Stock trading for beginners should begin with this. Register an account and put the funds which will be used to make the first time you buy penny stocks. The commissions are charged in all times, as there are some trading platforms which charge higher than others. Also, you should consider your requirements for trading when selecting the appropriate trading platform.

traders who have account for trading in other securities may utilize the same account for buying the penny stock. It is only necessary to examine the plan you've signed up for to determine the types of charges you'll face when you begin trading penny stocks.

Be aware of your investments

The price of penny stocks fluctuates quickly and investors need to be aware constantly so that they don't miss the chance to buy or sell their stock. You must keep an eye on every stock you've invested your money in throughout the day to be aware of when it is time to move. Buy when prices are at a low level and sell as soon as prices go up to ensure that you don't be unable to profit from selling.

It is also important to be aware of your portfolio's performance in order to see what you are doing and how badly you're doing each and every day. This can motivate you to do better, especially in the event that you're not performing very well.

The most important thing investors have to be aware of is that they should follow the same trading strategies throughout the entire time. Your strategy of trading was carefully crafted, with a lot of reasons, so switching it during trading because you're not seeing the anticipated returns is not a good decision. It is essential to remain consistently consistent when trading stocks in order to become an effective trader.

Continue to invest. The penny stocks aren't completely reliable. Therefore, an investor must be prepared to continue investing to make some profit from them. At times, you'll realize that certain stocks aren't performing well, and the only option in that moment is to dispose of the stock and then purchase those you believe are performing better. When you begin trading, you'll be able to observe what's happening on the market in order to become serious about trading and earn little gains.

Conclusion

I hope that this book was useful in helping you to understand the rapid-moving industry of penny stocks. Now you have the information to begin and should be confident about your capabilities. You've got the steps and the mental clarity that required me to learn for years. My earnings on traditional exchanges as well as penny stock exchanges have only increased over time, and that has been due to growing my knowledge and understanding and analysing my previous trades. Utilize the strategies in this book to find the right trade strategy to your advantage, as well as stay clear of the mistakes that traders fall into. I'm sure you'll succeed if you possess your mind set right, and are going into the market with the correct approach.

Next, you must begin exploring the different exchanges, to familiarize yourself with tools for analysis and to try out the type of trading that is the most profitable for you. Make a trade journal and then practice before deciding on a broker and begin trading money. Be sure to review your transactions and, based on your approach to trading and your personal preferences, set your limits accordingly. Be sure to follow the guidelines in this book and I'm confident that you will too have success with the penny-stock exchanges.

Thank you for your kind words and best wishes!

www.ingramcontent.com/pod-product-compliance
Lightning Source LLC
Chambersburg PA
CBHW071226210326
41597CB00016B/1963